The Daily Telegraph

TAX GUIDE 2011

The Daily Telegraph

TAX GUIDE 2011

PREPARED BY DAVID B. GENDERS, F.C.A.

CONSTABLE · LONDON

Constable & Robinson Ltd
3 The Lanchesters
162 Fulham Palace Road
London W6 9ER
www.constablerobinson.com

First published as *The Daily Telegraph Guide to Income Tax*, 1974

34th edition, completely revised, published by Constable,
an imprint of Constable & Robinson, 2011

ACKNOWLEDGEMENT
The HM Revenue & Customs forms reproduced in this
book are Crown copyright and are reproduced with
the permission of Her Majesty's Stationery Office.

A copy of the British Library Cataloguing in Publication
Data is available from the British Library

ISBN: 978-184901-646-9

Printed and bound in the EU

1 3 5 7 9 10 8 6 4 2

CONTENTS

Online filing of Returns. Input tax. Motor cars and fuel. Bad debts.
Special schemes for retailers. Flat Rate Scheme. Cash accounting.
Annual accounting. Penalties, surcharges and interest. Appeals.
Complaints.

About the author

David Genders has been writing *The Daily Telegraph Tax Guide* since 1982. A former partner of Sayers Butterworth LLP, Chartered Accountants in London, he joined the firm in 1965 as an apprentice before qualifying as a chartered accountant in 1970. After a career specialising in taxation, focusing on personal tax, David retired from his position of senior partner three years ago. He has, however, been retained by the practice as a tax consultant. David brings a wealth of knowledge and experience to the *Tax Guide*.

Away from tax affairs, David enjoys golf, gardening and walking, and still harbours an ambition to drive a steam train.

INTRODUCTION

We all want a better education for our children, an improved National Health Service, a more efficient and reliable transport system, less congestion on the roads and to feel safer and more secure in our homes and when we walk the streets. So who has to foot the bill for all these services? The Government, of course. And how does the Government raise the revenues to meet this expenditure? Mainly by taxing income, wealth, production and imports as well as collecting Social contributions from us. Any deficit from one year to the next is funded by borrowing.

The taxes covered in the *Guide* are:

- Income Tax – what we pay annually on our earnings and income from savings.

- Capital Gains Tax – paid only when we realize profits on sales of our assets.

- Inheritance Tax – chargeable on some lifetime gifts of capital and on the value of our Estates on death.

- Value Added Tax – included in the price of many goods and services we buy.

- National Insurance and Social Security – the contributions we have to pay based on our earnings or business profits and the various benefits, including the State Pension, we receive in return.

- Tax Credits – whether you are eligible and how to work out what you can claim.

For many people tax is both confusing and complicated. This book aims to:

- explain the basics of the taxes covered for the average taxpayer as straightforwardly as possible;

- help the reader have a better understanding of their tax affairs and, therefore, be able to take control;

- make staying within the law as easy as possible; and

- help cut tax bills with pointers to saving on tax.

This edition of the *Tax Guide* is primarily intended to cover the Self-Assessment tax year from 6 April 2010 to 5 April 2011 and is being published shortly after you should have received a Tax Return for this year.

The tax changes announced by the Chancellor of the Exchequer of the Coalition Government in his June 2010 and March 2011 Budgets are set out in the final chapter of the book.

I hope you benefit from the read.

1   YOU AND HMRC

Ask any taxpayer the question 'Would you like to pay less tax?' and I imagine that, almost without exception, the answer would be 'Yes'.

By the time you have finished reading this book I would like to think that you will have come across at least one way of saving tax, maybe:

- another allowance or relief you can claim;
- an expense that could be included in your business accounts; or
- a more tax-efficient structuring of your cash savings and investments.

But, first of all, you should have an understanding of the workings of the various HM Revenue & Customs (HMRC) departments responsible for the day-to-day running of our tax system.

HMRC was launched back in 2005 following the merger of the former departments of the Inland Revenue and HM Customs & Excise.

The Board of HMRC has overall authority for administering the fiscal legislation enacted by Government. Although there are a large number of specialist departments within HMRC, it is likely that your only contact with HMRC will be through the staff at your Tax Office and the Collector of Taxes.

Tax offices

Each tax office throughout the country is headed up by a Senior Officer with a full support staff. The tax affairs of employees and pensioners are looked after by the tax office that deals with the Pay-As-You-Earn affairs of their employer or pension fund. If you are self-employed you will find that the tax office responsible for your tax affairs is often local to your business address.

Currently there are the following types of tax office:

Service Office

It is your Service Office which:

- sends you a Tax Return to complete each year;

- processes your Return when you send it back;

- corrects any obvious or simple errors which you have made and sends you a notice detailing the amendments; and

- initially chases you up if you are late sending in your Return.

Service Offices are also responsible for:

- looking after all the day-to-day tax matters of the vast majority of taxpayers whose income is taxed under Pay-As-You-Earn and do not come within the system of Self-Assessment; and

- processing the business accounts of self-employed taxpayers.

As long as you comply with all your tax obligations and in a timely manner, your only involvement with HMRC will be confined to your Service Office.

Compliance Office

Often situated in the same office block as a Service Office each Compliance Office is responsible for:

- providing technical assistance to the local Service Office;

- investigating the Tax Returns and business accounts of those taxpayers selected for further attention; and

- beginning enforcement and recovery action of late Tax Returns or payments.

Wealthy Taxpayers

If you are one of the wealthiest taxpayers your tax affairs are looked after by the High Net Worth Unit (HNWU). It is intended that this new HNWU will:

- build relationships to help better understand these taxpayers and make it easier for them to get things right; and

- better tailor service delivery for these taxpayers through proactive engagement and by providing a single point of contact as well as a holistic approach for their tax affairs.

High-earning taxpayers, but whose affairs are otherwise largely uncomplicated, are dealt with by an HMRC office in Stockton-on-Tees.

Tax Enquiry Centre

The address and telephone number of your nearest Tax Enquiry Centre are in your local telephone book under HMRC. The functions of such offices are to:

- help with enquiries and provide assistance personally or over the telephone;

- accept payments of tax from taxpayers who prefer to pay locally; and

- supply forms, leaflets and helpsheets.

A list of the remaining helpful booklets on different aspects of our tax system published by HMRC (Revenue) is set out in Appendix 1 at the end of the book. Many of the leaflets have now been withdrawn and replaced by helpsheets which can be downloaded from the self-assessment area of the HMRC website.

The Collector of Taxes

The main tasks of HMRC Accounts Offices are to:

- bank payments of tax and National Insurance Contributions; and

- keep up-to-date accurate payments records.

If you need to telephone, write to or visit any of these offices please always give your name and reference number. You can find the address and telephone number on forms and letters that have been sent to you.

Business by telephone

If your tax affairs are handled by a Tax District which is part of a Contact Centre the following services are available to you by telephone:

- personal information such as changes of address or in your personal circumstances;

- employment details;

- claims to personal allowances;

- claims for either tax relief on flat-rate expenses (see Appendix 2 at the end of the book) or certain professional subscriptions to be included in the PAYE coding for the current year;

- employee benefits such as a company car, fuel for private motoring and medical insurance which affect your PAYE coding;

- notification of Gift Aid payments or contributions into your pension plan;

- other information such as the receipt of a State Pension;

- making certain amendments to your Self-Assessment Return; and

- dealing with tax repayments due to you.

In most cases nothing more will be needed from you, although the call may lead to further action by HMRC (for example, sending out a revised PAYE Coding Notice). Where your business cannot be completely dealt with by telephone, the HMRC officer will arrange to send you any necessary forms or follow-up material.

When you telephone do not be put off by any steps taken to establish your identity. Any such checks are for the purpose of safeguarding the privacy of your tax affairs.

Dealing with your Tax Office

On any straightforward matter, which does not come within the 'business by telephone' services, if you want a quick answer it is better to telephone your Tax Office. You will be put through to one of the Tax Inspector's assistants who should be able to help you with an enquiry about any of the following:

- general questions about Income Tax and Capital Gains Tax;

- specific questions affecting your own tax liability;

- help with completing Tax Returns and other HMRC forms; and

- requests for leaflets, forms and other HMRC information.

On more involved aspects of your tax affairs I recommend you put these in writing to your Tax Office. Occasionally you may want to make a visit to your Tax Office for a detailed discussion on a particular matter of your tax affairs. Where this is a long way from your home or place of work you can always visit a local HMRC office or your nearest Tax Enquiry Centre.

Whenever you telephone or write always remember to quote your reference number which is:

- your employer's PAYE reference; or

- your National Insurance Number; or

- if you are self-employed or pay tax at the higher rate, your Self-Assessment Unique Taxpayer Reference (UTR). This is a 10-digit number.

Enquiries

Once your Return has been processed by your Tax Office, it will undergo a comprehensive programme of checks. Any obvious errors, for example in your arithmetic, will be corrected and no further enquiries will probably be made. But enquiries will be started by your Tax Office if:

- something requires fuller explanation;

- there is a risk your Return may be incorrect; or

- your Return is selected for enquiry at random.

Normally HMRC have 12 months from the date that your Return is received by your tax office in which to tell you that it will be the subject of enquiries. However, the time limits for paper and online Returns differ slightly as illustrated by the following table for 2010/11 Returns.

Paper Returns

When filed	Enquiry window
On time – by 31 October 2011	12 months from the day the Return was filed.
Filed late	Up to, and including, the quarter day following the first anniversary of the date of filing the Return.

Online Returns

On time – by 31 January 2012	12 months from the day the Return was filed.
Filed late	Up to, and including, the quarter day following the first anniversary of the date of filing the Return.

Your Return will normally become final if your Tax Office has not raised any enquiries within the permitted time period. HMRC can only raise enquiries at a later date if they discover an error which they could not reasonably have been expected to be aware of from the information provided in, or with, your Return.

At the end of an enquiry into your Return HMRC will issue a closure notice which will include the making of any necessary adjustments to your Self-Assessment. You have 30 days in which to appeal against such amendments.

Any enquiries by your Tax Office should be conducted in accordance with the specific code of practice laid down by HMRC. If your Tax Return ever becomes the subject of an enquiry this may well be a time when you should be represented by a professional tax adviser.

Determinations

Not surprisingly HMRC has special powers to deal with taxpayers who are sent a Return but fail to complete it and submit it by the filing date. In such cases an offending taxpayer can expect HMRC to make a determination of his or her income and capital gains chargeable to tax to the best of their knowledge and belief. The actual amount of tax is based on estimates of:

- the taxpayer's allowances and reliefs; and

- tax deducted at source on earnings and savings income.

Any determination can be subsequently superseded by a Self-Assessment by the taxpayer or HMRC based on information provided by the taxpayer.

Assessments and appeals

In cases of fraud or neglect your Inspector of Taxes can raise an assessment to collect tax which should have been paid on a Self-Assessment.

You do, of course, have a right of appeal against:

- an assessment raised by your Tax Inspector; or

- an amendment to your Return following an enquiry.

The procedure for resolving your appeal starts with a hearing before an Independent Tribunal of expert tax judges and/or panel members. It can then move on to the courts and ultimately to the House of Lords.

Prosecutions

An important role of HMRC is to deter fraud. They will prosecute in serious cases in all areas of the tax system. Cases selected for prosecution involve a wide range of offences. However, a case is more likely to be considered for prosecution if it contains features such as:

- falsification of documents;
- lying during an investigation;
- conspiracy; or
- discovery of false documents made during an earlier investigation.

Your Charter

HMRC make sure that money is available to fund the UK Public Services by collecting the taxes and duties as laid down by Parliament.

HMRC want to:

- give you a service that is evenhanded, accurate and based on mutual trust and respect; and
- make it as easy as they can for you to get things right.

This Charter explains what you can expect from HMRC and what HMRC can expect from you.

Your Rights

What you can expect from HMRC:

Respect you

HMRC will:

- treat you with courtesy and consideration;
- listen to your concerns;
- answer your questions in a way you can understand;
- try to understand your circumstances;
- make you aware of your rights, including your right to appeal their decisions; and
- tell you how to exercise your right to appeal against their decisions.

Help and support you to get things right

HMRC will:

- provide information that helps you understand what you have to do and when you have to do it;
- provide information that clearly explains the taxes, duties, exemptions, allowances, reliefs and tax credits that they are responsible for;
- process the information you give them as quickly and accurately as they can; and
- put mistakes right as soon as they can.

Treat you as honest

Unless HMRC have a good reason not to, they will:

- presume you are telling them the truth;
- accept that you will pay what you owe and only claim what you are entitled to;
- explain why they need to ask you questions and why they have decided to check your records; and
- only question what you tell them if they have good reason to.

Treat you even-handedly

HMRC will:

- act within the law and their published guidance;

- help you understand your legal rights;

- explain what you can do if you disagree with their decisions or want to make a complaint;

- provide you with information in a way that meets your particular needs; and

- consider any financial difficulties you may be having.

Be professional and act with integrity

HMRC will:

- act with integrity;

- make sure that you are dealt with by people who have the right level of expertise;

- make decisions in accordance with the law and published guidance and explain them clearly to you;

- respond to your enquiries and resolve any problems as soon as they can; and

- let you know how appeals, investigations or complaints are progressing.

Tackle people who deliberately break the rules and challenge those who bend the rules

HMRC will:

- identify people who are not paying what they owe or claiming more than they should;

- recover the money they owe and charge interest and penalties where appropriate;

- distinguish between legitimately trying to pay the lowest amount and bending rules through tax avoidance; and

- use their powers reasonably.

Protect your information and respect your privacy

HMRC will:

- protect information they obtain, receive or hold about you;

- explain why they need information, if you ask them to;

- only allow their staff to see information when they need it to do their job;

- give you the information they hold about you when you ask for it, as long as the law lets them;

- only share or release information about you when the law lets them and they need to; and

- respect your legal rights when they visit premises.

Accept that someone else can represent you

HMRC will:

- respect your representative's right to act for you and deal with them appropriately.

Do all they can to keep the cost of dealing with them as low as possible

HMRC will:

- try to make their services straightforward and easy to access;

- make it as cheap as they can for you to contact them;

- explain clearly what they need from you;

- do their best to give you complete, accurate and consistent advice; and

- do their best to get things right first time.

Your obligations

What HMRC expect from you:

Be honest

HMRC expect you to:

- be truthful, open and act within the law;
- give them accurate information;
- give them all the relevant facts; and
- tell them as soon as you can if you think you have made a mistake.

Respect their staff

HMRC expect you to:

- be polite; and
- accept that they will not tolerate rude or abusive behaviour.

Take care to get things right

HMRC expect you to:

- take reasonable care when you complete tax returns and fill out forms;
- send them tax returns and forms on time;
- make payments on time;
- respond in good time if they ask you to do something;
- talk to them if there is anything that you are not sure about or if you are having difficulty meeting your obligations;
- tell them if you have any particular needs so they can take them into account;
- tell them about any changes in your circumstances that will affect your payments or claims; and
- keep adequate records that support what you tell them and hold them for as long as the law says you need to.

Complaints

Any complaint should, first of all, be made to the Tax Office with which you are dealing. Address your letter to the Officer in Charge, describe the complaint (slow service, constant mistakes) and the remedy you want (an apology, compensation).

Most complaints about HMRC's handling of people's tax affairs are satisfactorily settled by their Tax Office. Where taxpayers are not satisfied with the response from their office, they can complain to:

- senior local management;

- HMRC's Head Office;

- a Member of Parliament; or

- the Parliamentary Commissioner for Administration.

Taxpayers who are still dissatisfied can put their case to the HMRC Adjudicator, who will consider complaints about the way in which HMRC:

- has handled someone's tax affairs – for example, complaints about excessive delay, errors, discourtesy; or

- has exercised discretion.

The Adjudicator will review all the facts and try to reach a decision as soon as possible. HMRC normally accepts this decision except where there are exceptional circumstances. The Board of HMRC receives an annual report from the Adjudicator which serves as a useful mechanism in identifying problem areas and required changes.

Changes in legislation

Every year in March or early April the Chancellor of the Exchequer makes his annual Budget Statement. This is often preceded by a Pre-Budget Report, usually in the previous November or December. Not only does he use these occasions to report on the nation's finances, but they are the times when he tells us about:

- tax rates and allowances for the following year; and

- new or amending legislation to our tax laws.

Resulting legislative changes are published in a Finance Bill. Its various clauses are debated by Parliament and occasionally amended. Subsequently, the Bill is passed by both Houses of Parliament before receiving Royal Assent. It is then published as a Finance Act.

When the law is either unclear or ambiguous HMRC will issue a Statement of Practice indicating how they intend to interpret it. There are also times when HMRC does not seek to go by the strict letter of the law. These are gathered together and published as a list of Extra-Statutory Concessions.

2 TAX RATES AND ALLOWANCES

For most of us our annual tax bill is simply dependent on:

- tax bands and rates; and
- the allowances and credits we can claim.

Income Tax rates

Under our tax system, the tax (or fiscal) year runs from each 6 April to the following 5 April.

The rates of tax for 2010/11 are:

Band of Taxable Income	Rate of Tax	Tax on Band	Cumulative Tax
£	%	£	£
0–37,400	20	7,480.00	7,480.00
37,401–150,000	40	45,040.00	52,520.00
over 150,000	50		

The rate of 20% is known as the basic rate. Tax at 40% is referred to as the higher rate. The additional rate refers to tax at the new 50% level.

Income from dividends is taxed at:

- 10% on dividend income within the basic rate limit of £37,400;
- 32.5% within the higher rate tax band; and
- 42.5% above the higher rate limit.

Starting rate of savings income

A lower tax rate of 10% is charged on your savings income.

- of up to £2,440; but

- after taking off your personal allowance.

Savings income is that such as interest on a bank or building society account, but not dividends.

However, because earnings and pensions are treated as the first slice of taxable income the number of taxpayers who will benefit from this lower 10% starting rate on savings income will be few and far between.

Florence Kirk had income from pensions of £7,000 and from savings of £3,000 during 2010/11. She paid Income Tax of £513.50 calculated as follows:

	£
Total Income	10,000.00
Less: Personal allowance	6,475.00
Taxable Income	£3,525.00
Income Tax payable	£
£1,915 @ 10%	191.50
£1,610 @ 20%	322.00
	£513.50

Florence's personal allowance is first of all set against her pensions of £7,000 which restricts the amount of her savings income taxable at 10% by £525.

Allowances

You can reduce the income on which you pay tax by claiming any of the allowances to which you are entitled.

The rates of the various tax allowances for 2010/11 are:

	£
Personal	
aged under 65	*6,475
aged 65–74	**9,490
aged 75 and over	**9,640
Married Couples	
aged 75 and over	***6,965
minimum amount	***2,670
Relief for Blind person (each)	1,890

* The personal allowance reduces at the rate of £1 for every £2 of income in excess of £100,000.

** The personal age and married couple's allowances come down by £1 for every £2 of income above a specified limit – £22,900 for 2010/11.

*** Indicates where tax relief is restricted to 10%.

Allowances, other than the married couple's, are deducted from total income in working out the amount of Income Tax you pay each year. Tax relief for the married couple's allowance is given as a deduction from tax payable.

Indexation

Unless Parliament decides otherwise most allowances and the tax rate bands are linked to annual inflation increases. This movement is in line with the increase in the Retail Prices Index (RPI) during the year to the end of September prior to the tax year and applies to:

- the bands of income taxable at the starting and basic rates;
- the personal allowances;
- the married couple's allowances;
- blind person's relief; and
- the income limit for age allowances.

Personal allowance

Every man, woman or child, single or married, resident in the UK can claim the personal allowance. This is set against total income on which Income Tax is payable such as:

- a wage, salary or business profits;
- an occupational and/or a State Pension; and
- income from investments.

During 2010/11, Richard West, a married man in his early 40s, earned £26,000 from his job. His tax liability for the year is £3,905.00, worked out as follows:

	£
Salary	26,000
Less: Personal allowance	6,475
Taxable income	£19,525
Income Tax payable	
£19,525 @ 20%	£3,905.00

Paul Frost received remuneration, including benefits, of £107,000 during 2010/11. His tax liability for the year amounted to £34,130.00, worked out as follows:

	£
Remuneration	107,000
Less: Personal allowance	2,975
Taxable income	£104,025
Income Tax payable	
£37,400 @ 20%	7,480.00
£66,625 @ 40%	26,650.00
	£34,130.00

Paul's personal allowance for the year is reduced by £3,500 ($^1/_2$ x £107,000 – £100,000) from £6,475 to £2,975.

As the table on page 16 shows, the amount of your annual personal allowance depends on your age. A pensioner, aged 65 years or over for part or all of the tax year, is eligible for the personal age allowance. There is an enhanced personal age allowance for elderly taxpayers who are over 74 years old during part or all of the tax year.

Married couple's allowance

A married couple living together can benefit from the married couple's allowance so long as one spouse is at least 75 years old at some stage in the tax year. For couples married before 5 December 2005 it is the husband who should make the claim. Thereafter the allowance is given to the spouse with the higher income. This option is also available, by election, to couples married up to 4 December 2005.

Eric Black was 78 years old in 2010/11. His younger wife, Myra, celebrated her 63rd birthday the same year. They are entitled to allowances of £16,605 and £6,475 as follows:

	Eric	Myra
	£	£
Personal age/personal	9,640	6,475
Married couple's	6,965	—
Total allowances	£16,605	£6,475

The amount of the married couple's allowance in the year of marriage depends upon the time in the year that the wedding takes place. The allowance is reduced by one-twelfth for every complete month from 6 April up to the day of the marriage.

Percy Hughes, aged 77, married his wife, Barbara, aged 67, on 6 November 2010. He receives an allowance of £2,903 for 2010/11 worked out as follows:

	£
Married couple's allowance	6,965
Less: Reduction	
$7/12 \times £6,965$	4,062
2010/11 Allowance	£2,903

There is no reduction in the married couple's allowance for a year when:

- couples separate;
- couples divorce; or
- one spouse dies.

A widow is entitled to any unused part of the married couple's allowance for the year in which she loses her husband.

A wife does not need her husband's consent to claim one half of the minimum amount of the married couple's allowance, £1,335 for 2010/11. Alternatively, a married couple can jointly elect for the wife to receive the full minimum amount of the allowance, £2,670 for 2010/11. Such an election:

- must be made using HMRC Form 18;

- must normally be made before the start of the tax year for which it is to apply (except in the year of marriage when the newly-weds can submit a notice dealing with the reduced married couple's allowance for that year); and

- once made carries on from year to year until changed by the couple.

Without the above election the husband is entitled to the full married couple's allowance. But, if he is on a low income and cannot make full use of this allowance, he can transfer any excess allowance to his wife by completing Form 575.

James Lucas, who is in his early 80s, had income from pensions of £11,800 in 2010/11. His wife, Mary, who is 25 years younger than James is still working and earned a salary of £13,700 in 2010/11. She elected to receive one half of the basic married couple's allowance.

James and Mary have been married for many years and have opted not to come within the rules applying to couples marrying on or after 5 December 2005.

James does not pay any tax for 2010/11 as follows:

	£
Pension	11,800
Less: Personal allowance	9,640
Taxable income	£2,160
Income Tax payable	
£2,160 @ 20%	432.00
Less: Relief for married couple's allowance £6,965 – ($^1/_2$ x £2,670) = £5,630 @ 10% but restricted to	432.00
	–

Mary has a tax bill for the year of £1,311.50 as follows:

	£
Salary	13,700
Less: Personal allowance	6,475
Taxable income	£7,225
Income Tax payable	
£7,225 @ 20%	1,445.00
Less: Relief for married couple's allowance £1,335 ($^1/_2$ x £2,670) @ 10%	133.50
	£1,311.50

The unused part of James's married couple's allowance amounts to £1,310. By making a claim, this can be transferred to Mary thereby reducing her tax bill by £131 (£1,310 @ 10%) from £1,311.50 to £1,180.50.

Civil partners

Same-sex couples can now have legal recognition of their relationship by forming a Civil Partnership. This is an equality measure for same-sex couples who are unable to marry.

Since Civil Partnership is a parallel status to marriage, the tax system has been adapted so that the various rules dealing with the taxation of married couples now also apply to civil partners.

Long-standing partners, Rex Gardner and Gerald Sullivan, entered into a civil partnership on 2 January 2010. They are both in their late 70s. Gerald, who has the higher income, can claim the married couple's allowance of £6,965 for 2010/11.

Age allowances – income limit

The purpose of the personal age and married couples allowances is to assist those pensioners on low and modest incomes. It follows, therefore, that these allowances are restricted when total income, after permitted reliefs and deductions, exceeds a specified limit – £22,900 for 2010/11. The reduction is £1 for each £2 by which total income is more than the annual stated limit. However:

- the reduced personal allowance cannot come to less than £6,475; and

- there is a minimum amount of £2,670 for the married couple's allowance.

The personal age allowance decreases first. When it comes to calculating any restriction to the married couple's allowance:

- It is worked out on the income of the husband or the spouse/civil partner with the higher income, as the case may be.

- It is not affected by the wife's income or that of the other civil partner no matter how much it is.

It follows that any benefit of the higher personal age allowance is lost for a pensioner aged 65–74 when income exceeds £28,930 increasing to £29,230 for a claimant over age 74.

The upper income limits beyond which the married couple's allowance reduces to the minimum amount for 2010/11 are:

Claimant's Age	Wife's/Partner's Age (Over 74)
	£
Under 65	**31,490**
65–74	**37,520**
Over 74	**37,820**

An elderly couple, Andrew Dawson, aged 80, and his wife Monica, aged 77, whose income amounted to £30,000 and £24,000 respectively during 2010/11 paid Income Tax of £4,047.00 and £2,982.00 respectively, worked out as follows:

		Andrew	Monica
		£	£
Income			
	State Pensions	5,077	2,802
	Pensions from former employers	21,923	19,998
	Building Society Interest	3,000	1,200
		30,000	24,000
	Less: Personal allowance	6,475	9,090
	Taxable Income	£23,525	£14,910
Income Tax payable			
	£23,525/£14,910 @ 20%	4,705.00	2,982.00
	Less: Relief for married couple's allowance – £6,580 @ 10%	658.00	—
		£4,047.00	£2,982.00

Andrew does not get any benefit from the personal age allowance as his income is more than £29,230. Monica's personal age allowance of £9,640 is reduced by £550 = 0.5 x £1,100 (£24,000 – income limit of £22,900).

The married couple's allowance of £6,965 is initially restricted by £3,550 = 0.5 x (£30,000 – £22,900). But Andrew's loss of personal allowance of £3,165 limits the loss of relief to £385 (from £6,965 to £6,580).

Blind person's relief

This relief is given to a registered blind person. Where both husband and wife or both civil partners are blind each of them can claim the relief. If either of them is on a low income and unable to use up his or her relief, any unused part can be transferred to the other even if he or she is not blind.

When a taxpayer first becomes entitled to this special relief, by being registered blind, the relief will also be given for the previous tax year if, at the time, the individual had received the necessary proof of blindness needed to qualify for registration. This concession prevents individuals losing out as a result of any delays in the registration process.

3   TAX CREDITS

To qualify for Tax Credits you must be:

- aged 16 or over; and

- usually living in the United Kingdom.

Married couples, couples living together as partners and civil partners must submit a single joint application.

Both Tax Credits are dependent on the incomes of the claimants.

Child Tax Credit

Child Tax Credit (CTC) is:

- available to individuals responsible for at least one child or qualifying young person; and

- paid by direct transfer to the bank account of the person (usually the mother) mainly responsible for the care of the child or children.

A child is a person under 16 years old or in the case of a 16-year-old teenager, until 1 September next after their 16th birthday. A qualifying young person is someone who is:

- no longer a child;

- under 20 years old; and

- in full-time education, usually at a school or college; or

- on an approved training course.

CTC is made up of the following elements:

Rates for 2010/11	Annual	Weekly
	£	£
Family element	545.00	10.48
Family element, baby addition (first year only)	545.00	10.48
Child element (each child)	2,300.00	44.23
Disability element	2,715.00	52.21
Severe disability element	1,095.00	21.05

Working Tax Credit

The Working Tax Credit (WTC) can be claimed by individuals who are:

- employed or self-employed;

- over age 24, without children, and usually work for at least 30 hours a week; or

- usually undertake paid work for at least 16 hours a week, are aged 16 and over and either responsible for at least one child or disabled person.

Recipients of WTC may also qualify for assistance with the costs of childcare. In such circumstances the childcare element of WTC is paid with entitlement to CTC, to the person responsible for the care of the child or children.

WTC comprises the following elements:

Rates for 2010/11	Annual	Weekly
	£	£
Basic entitlement	1,920.00	36.92
Additional couples, and lone parent, element	1,890.00	36.34
30 hour element	790.00	15.19
Disability element	2,570.00	49.42
Severe disability element	1,095.00	21.05
50 plus return to work payment, for 16–29 hours	1,320.00	25.38
50 plus return to work payment, for 30+ hours	1,965.00	37.78
Childcare element		
– maximum eligible cost		300.00
– maximum eligible cost for one child		175.00
Percentage of eligible cost covered		80%

Payment

HMRC pay both CTC and WTC to the main carer at either weekly or four-weekly intervals. Where there is a joint claim, the couple can jointly nominate the main carer. If they fail to do so:

- HMRC will make the decision; and

- nominate the main carer, who will usually be the mother or the person receiving Child Benefit.

Tapering

Tax Credits taper away at a rate of 39% for each £1 of family income over a threshold of £6,420 (£16,190 where no WTC is claimed). The first £300 of income from pensions, savings and property is excluded. The order of reduction is:

- Working Tax Credit;

- childcare element; and

- child elements of Child Tax Credit.

The family element and baby addition of CTC are tapered at a different rate by reference to:

- a second threshold of £50,000; and

- a different withdrawal rate of 1 in 15.

Sharon and Ken Bailey have three children, two sons aged 8 and 6 and a baby daughter born on 21 November 2010.

Ken works full time and earns a salary of £25,000. Sharon stays at home to look after the children. Before tapering their total entitlement to Tax Credits for 2010/11 is:

	£	£
Working Tax Credit		
Basic entitlement	1,920.00	
Additional couples element	1,890.00	
30 hour element	790.00	
	———	4,600.00
Child Tax Credit		
Family element	545.00	
Baby addition	545.00	
Child element (3)	6,900.00	
	———	7,990.00

The effect of tapering is to reduce entitlement by £7,246.20 (being 39% x £25,000 – £6,420). As a result Ken receives no WTC and the CTC paid to Sharon is reduced by £2,646.20 to £5,343.80.

Alison Baldwin is a single parent. She looks after her two daughters aged 4 and 2. She pays £260 per week for childcare costs. Alison is a successful businesswoman earning a salary of £35,000 per annum. Her Tax Credits for 2010/11 work out at £9,415 as follows:

	£	£
Working Tax Credit		
Basic entitlement	1,920.00	
Lone parent element	1,890.00	
30 hour element	790.00	
Childcare element	*10,816.00	
		15,416.00
Child Tax Credit		
Child element (2)	4,600.00	
Family element	545.00	
		5,145.00
		20,561.00
Less: Taper 39% x £28,580 (£35,000 – £6,420)		11,146.00
Total Credits		£9,415.00

* £208 per week being 80% of the cost of £260 per week.

Annual Renewal

From around April each year onwards an existing claimant will receive a letter telling him or her how to finalise the award for the year just finished and make a claim for the following year. You have until 31 July in which to provide the information requested. Once your reply has been processed you will receive a notice about your final Tax Credit for that year.

If you have received too much Tax Credit you will be expected to refund the excess. This will usually be done by restricting the award for the following year.

If you have been paid too little Tax Credit you will receive the extra as a single payment.

Changes in Circumstances

Once a claimant has been granted Tax Credits, even for a nil amount, he or she has a duty to advise HMRC within one month of certain stipulated changes in circumstances which are:

- the number of children for which support can be claimed;

- in work status;

- marriage, moving in to live with a partner or entering a civil partnership;

- separation;

- discontinuing payment to a childcare provider for at least four weeks continuously; and/or

- a drop of more than £10 a week in costs of childcare, again for at least four weeks in a row.

There may be other changes in circumstances, such as the birth of a child that should be notified to HMRC particularly to avoid losing out on an award.

Income Disregard

Not only is a claimant's entitlement to tax credits continuously adjusted by alterations in lifestyle circumstances but it is also affected by changes to income in the award period, namely a tax year. Therefore, when a claimant's income drops, a higher award can be immediately requested. Conversely when income increases the amount of the award will come down.

It is, however, provided that a claimant's income for tax credit purposes can increase by as much as £25,000 in a claim year, compared to the previous year, without any reduction in entitlement. This gives more certainty to claimants that their payments will not suddenly be decreased when their income goes up during an award period.

Penalties and Interest

The following penalties can be charged:

Offence	*Penalty*
Failure to notify a change of in-year circumstances or to provide information or evidence required by HMRC.	An initial penalty of £300 followed by penalties of up to £60 per day for continuing failure.
Over-claiming Tax Credits	Variable depending on mistake or misunderstanding, failure to take reasonable care, serious or deliberate error.
Making negligent or fraudulent claims, statements or declarations.	Up to £3,000

Interest may also be charged by HMRC where Tax Credits are overpaid, wholly or partly resulting from a claimant failing to take reasonable care, neglect or fraud.

Help and Advice

If you would like help or advice about tax credits:

- you can phone the Helpline on 0845 300 3900 (England, Scotland & Wales) or 0845 603 2000 (Northern Ireland);

- go online to www.hmrc.gov.uk/taxcredits;

- visit a local advice service such as a Citizens' Advice Bureau who may be able to help.

Changes from 6 April 2011

- The baby addition of CTC is discontinued.

- The rate at which Tax Credits taper away goes up from 39% to 41%.

- Where no WTC is claimed, the income threshold for tapering reduces from £16,190 to £15,860.

- The second income and withdrawal rates change from £50,000 to £40,000 and 6.67% to 41% respectively.

- The increase in income which is disregarded in a claim year drops by £10,000 to £15,000.

4 INTEREST PAYMENTS AND OTHER OUTGOINGS

The opportunities for claiming tax relief on interest paid on borrowings are few and far between. They are for:

- the purchase, in certain circumstances, of life annuities if you are aged 65 or over;

- buying a share in:

  — an employee-controlled company;

  — a close company (i.e. controlled by five or fewer shareholders), or lending capital to it;

  — a partnership, or contributing capital to a partnership, if you are a partner;

- buying plant and machinery for use in your job or partnership so long as the plant and machinery attracts capital allowances for tax purposes (see Chapter 7).

Interest is also allowable for tax purposes on a replacement loan where the interest on existing borrowings qualifies for tax relief.

It is important to understand that the purpose for which a loan is advanced governs whether the interest on it will be eligible for tax relief. How the loan is secured is not relevant.

Apart from interest on a loan to acquire buy-to-let property, the interest on which tax relief is due is deducted from your total income in the year of payment. It cannot be spread over the period of accrual, nor can tax relief be claimed if the interest is not actually paid.

Home annuity loans

Interest on a loan taken out before 9 March 1999 to purchase an annuity (an investment providing a fixed or increasing annual sum) from an insurance company still attracts tax relief at 23% provided:

- the borrower was at least 65 years old at the time the annuity was purchased;

- not less than 90% of the loan on which the interest is payable went towards buying an annuity for life; or

- security for the loan is the borrower's main residence.

The maximum loan on which tax relief is allowed is £30,000. Where a loan exceeds this limit tax relief is given on the proportion of the total interest payable equivalent to the £30,000 limit. Income Tax at the special rate of 23% will be deducted at source by the insurance company in working out the regular payments to be made by the borrower.

Buy-to-let property

Interest on a loan taken out to buy, improve or alter a property which you let out is tax deductible. The interest paid each year is set against the rental income from the property and any other properties which you are renting out as part of your income from property business. If the interest paid exceeds the rents less expenses in the same tax year, the excess cannot be set against your other income. The loss can only be carried forward for offset against rental income in future years.

Lionel Foster acquired a buy-to-let flat in 1998 with the assistance of a mortgage of £120,000. His rents less expenses came to £2,500 and £11,000 during 2009/10 and 2010/11 respectively.

	2009/10	2010/11	
	£	£	£
Rents less expenses	2,500		11,000
Less: Loan interest paid	6,000	6,500	
Loss carried forward	£3,500	3,500	
			10,000
2010/11 Net rental income			£1,000

Business loans

Interest on any borrowings by your business can count as a deduction from your business profits for tax purposes. Provided that the borrowed money is used for business purposes it does not matter whether the interest is paid on:

- a loan taken out for some specific purpose; or

- borrowings because your bank account goes overdrawn.

Interest you pay will also qualify for tax relief where you need to borrow to:

- buy an asset, such as a car or a piece of machinery, for use in your business. The tax allowable interest will be restricted by the extent of any private usage; or

- purchase a share in a partnership of which you are about to become a member, or to contribute capital for use in its business.

Perhaps, however, you have business connections with a private company? Interest paid on a loan raised so you can either buy shares in the company, or lend it money for use in its business, is tax deductible. You must either:

- own at least 5% of the company's share capital; or

- hold at least some shares in the company and spend the greater part of your time working in the business.

Employees who need to borrow to buy shares in their company, as part of an employee buy-out, are allowed tax relief on the interest paid on their borrowings.

Gift Aid

Gift Aid is an Income Tax relief for cash gifts, without limit, by individuals to charities. Under Gift Aid a charity can claim back tax from HMRC on your cash donation. For donations made on or after 6 April 2008, when the basic rate of tax was reduced from 22% to 20%, charities can claim repayments:

- at the basic rate of 20%; and

- they are also entitled to transitional relief worth 3p for every £1 donated under Gift Aid. This transitional relief will be paid on all donations between 6 April 2008 and 5 April 2011.

You can:

- give any amount, large or small, regularly or as a one-off donation;
- pay by cash, cheque, postal order, standing order, direct debit, or by using your credit or debit card.

For your donation to qualify under Gift Aid you must:

- pay at least as much tax in the tax year in which you make your cash gifts as the charities will reclaim on them; and
- make a declaration to the charity, either orally or in writing, that you want your donation to be regarded as made under Gift Aid.

If you pay tax at either the 40% or 50% rates, you can claim tax relief on your Gift Aid donations. This is worked out on the difference between the top rate at which you pay and the basic rate of tax.

Norman Walton gave donations totalling £1,560 under Gift Aid in 2010/11. Norman is a higher rate taxpayer so he can reduce his tax bill by £390 as follows:

	£
Grossed-up donations – $£1,560 \times \dfrac{100}{80} =$	1,950
Tax relief thereon at 40%	780
Less: Deducted when making donations	390
Reduction in Income Tax payable	£390

You can claim to carry back donations so they are treated as if paid in the previous tax year. For example, donations made after 5 April 2011; and

- before 31 January 2012; or
- the date when you send your 2010/11 Tax Return to your Tax Office (if earlier),

can be carried back to 2010/11 so you get the tax relief in that year rather than in the year of payment.

Self-Assessment Tax Returns include a facility for individuals to give a tax repayment to charity. The main features of this arrangement are:

- you can choose a charity from the list published by HMRC;

- you are under no obligation to donate the whole repayment to charity. You can stipulate how much you want to give; and

- donations made this way can also be under Gift Aid.

If you do not pay tax, Gift Aid is not for you.

Gifts of assets to charities

You can claim relief from Income Tax at your top rate of tax for the full market value of any gifts of shares, securities or land and buildings to charities at the time of the gift. The assets that qualify for this type of tax relief are:

- shares or securities listed on a recognized Stock Exchange;

- shares or securities dealt in on any market in the UK that is designated for this purpose by HMRC;

- units in an authorized unit trust;

- shares in an open-ended investment company;

- an interest in an offshore fund; and

- land and buildings.

This Income Tax relief is in addition to exemption from Capital Gains Tax on such assets given to charities.

Jennifer Pickard pays tax at the higher rate of 40% on a substantial part of her income. In September 2010 she decided to give shares in a quoted company valued at £5,000 to a registered charity. The taxable capital gain on the shares would have been £3,000 if she had sold them. Jennifer saves tax of £2,840 as follows:

	£
Reduction in Income Tax (40% x £5,000)	2,000
Capital Gains Tax not payable on the gain (28% x £3,000)	840
2010/11 Maximum tax saving	£2,840

Payroll giving

If you are in employment there may be another way that you can make tax-efficient gifts to charity. But, first of all, you need to enquire of your employer whether it participates in such an arrangement through a Charity Arrangement approved by HMRC. If so you can ask your employer to make regular deductions from your salary which, as part of the scheme, will be passed on to the charities of your choice. You will receive full Income Tax relief on such donations. There is no limit to the amount you can contribute this way each year.

5   WORKING IN EMPLOYMENT

Most of us have worked for somebody else at some stage in our lives either on a full-time, or part-time basis.

Am I employed?

Generally speaking you are regarded as employed:

- if you work for the same organization from day to day; and
- you do not have the risks associated with the running of a business.

If the answer is 'yes' to most of the following questions then you will correctly have been categorized as having employee status:

- do you have to do the work yourself?
- can you be told where to work, when to work, how to work and what to do?
- can you be moved from job to job?
- do you have to work a set number of hours?
- are you paid a regular wage or salary?
- can you get additional pay for overtime and a bonus?
- are you entitled to holiday pay and sickness pay when you are away from work unwell?
- are you responsible for managing anyone else engaged by your employer?

Earnings

The earnings from an employment on which Income Tax is payable are:

- a salary or wage;
- a bonus;

- overtime;

- commission;

- tips or gratuities;

- holiday or sick pay;

- part-time earnings;

- director's salary or fees; and

- benefits-in-kind.

The Pay-As-You-Earn (PAYE) system

The mechanism for collecting the tax due on earnings from an employment is the PAYE system. It is the responsibility of employers to deduct Income Tax from the earnings of their employees. The total deductions must be paid over to HMRC every month. The PAYE deducted from an employee's earnings is regarded as a credit against the total tax payable by the employee for that tax year. Each employee's individual allowances and reliefs are taken into account by the employer in working out the amount of tax to deduct from the employee's salary or wage. This is possible because HMRC issues all employers with a code number for each employee.

Code numbers

Every employee's annual PAYE Coding Notice sets out:

- on the first lines, the total tax allowances due; and

- on the left-hand side on the lines below, the amounts taken away from the allowances.

The PAYE system allows for the net allowances to be spread evenly throughout the tax year in working out the deductions for Income Tax so as to avoid any substantial variation to the amount of the regular salary cheque or pay packet.

All things being equal this system should ensure that the right amount of tax is deducted from your earnings each year. However, it can only work properly and effectively if you promptly tell your Tax Office of changes in your personal circumstances that affect any of the entries on your Notice of

Coding. For example, most Coding Notices for the 2011/12 tax year, beginning on 6 April 2011, were sent out during the early part of the year. This is before your Tax Office will have received your 2011 Tax Return, stating your income, capital gains, reliefs and allowances for the year to 5 April 2011. It follows, therefore, that the information on which all 2011/12 code numbers have been based is out of date. This is why it is important that you check your code number for 2011/12 and tell your Tax Office if:

- alterations are required to your allowances of reliefs;

- you have changed jobs or ceased to be employed;

- you have started receiving a pension;

- there has been a big change in your income; or

- you have moved home.

Your tax allowances for 2011/12 should be correct as all the Income Tax allowances for this year were released by the Treasury last December. These are:

		£
Personal		7,475
Age	Personal: age 65–74	9,940
	Personal: age 75 and over	10,090
	Married couples – maximum	7,295
	Married couples – minimum	2,670

If the 2011 Budget contains any other changes affecting your 2011/12 Coding Notice your Tax Office will send you details together with an amended Notice.

Below is an illustration of Simon Black's 2011/12 Notice of Coding.

(ab) **HM Revenue & Customs**

PAYE Coding Notice

Tax code for tax year

2011-2012

Please keep all your coding notices. You may need to refer to them if you have to fill in a tax return. Please also quote your tax reference and National Insurance number if you contact us

MR S BLACK
12 CHURCH RISE
BROADWOOD
PT3 8ZL

H M REVENUE & CUSTOMS
BROADWOOD DISTRICT
FOREST HOUSE
BROADWOOD
PT3 9LB

Telephone	Date of issue
01397 615594	3 Feb 2011

Tax reference	National Insurance number
28/B604	BZ 62 24 17 A

Dear MR S BLACK

Your tax code for the year 6th April 2011 to 5th April 2012 is 135L

You need a tax code so Broadwood Engineers Ltd can work out how much tax to take off the payments they make to you from 6 April 2011. It is important to make sure that we have got your tax right. The **Notes** will help you do this. If you contact us we will need your National Insurance number and tax reference. Please keep your coding notices; you may need them if we send you a tax return.

Here is how we worked it out			
your personal allowance		£7475	(see Note 1 below)
car benefit	-£2040		(see Note 2 below)
car fuel benefit	- £3060		
medical insurance	- £600		(see Note 3 below)
reduction to collect unpaid tax £76.00	- £420	- £6120	(see Note 4 below)
a tax free amount of		£1355	(see Note 5 below)

We turn £1355 into tax code 135L to send to Broadwood Engineers Ltd. They should use this code to take off the right amount of tax each time they pay you from 6 April 2011. We tell Broadwood Engineers Ltd what your tax code is but we do not tell them how it is worked out.

Simon is a married man, with two young children, who does not pay tax above the basic rate of 20%. On the first line of the Notice is Simon's personal allowance for 2011/12 of £7,475. The amounts taken away from Simon's allowances are on the lines below. These are:

- The first three deductions are the taxable figures of the benefits-in-kind of a company car, free fuel for private motoring and private medical insurance cover provided to Simon and his family by his employer. The Income Tax payable by Simon on these benefits is, therefore, collected by restricting his allowances by the taxable amount of the benefits.

- The last deduction is for tax of £84.00 underpaid in 2009/10. For a number of reasons the allowances given, or deductions included, in Simon's Notice of Coding may turn out not to be always totally correct. If, as a result, tax is underpaid, this is usually collected in a subsequent year by restricting allowances in the coding. In the illustration a restriction of Simon's 2011/12 allowances by £420 will enable HMRC to collect the underpayment of £84.00 (£420 @ 20%) from him.

The combined effect of these adjustments is to leave Simon with allowances of just £1,355 to be set against his salary for 2011/12. His code number is 135L. It is not difficult to see that there is a direct link between Simon's allowances and his code number. The suffix letter added to the coding is a way of identifying the category into which a taxpayer falls.

- L   is for a code with the basic personal allowance;

- P   is for a code with the personal allowance for those aged 65–74;

- Y   is the code if you are due the personal allowance for age 75 and over; and

- T   applies in most other cases, for example:

  — if you ask your Tax Office not to use any of the letters listed above; or

  — if there are items in the coding which need to be reviewed.

There are also a number of other codes:

- BR   this tells your employer to deduct tax at the basic rate.

- NT   means that no tax will be deducted.

- DO   tax will be deducted at the higher rate of 40%.

- DI   tax will be taken off at the additional rate of 50%.

- Prefix K – a K code is given to employees whose total deductions including taxable benefits exceed their personal allowances. The amount of the negative allowances is then added to the pay on which tax is payable. The system of K codes ensures that taxpayers pay all the tax due on their excess benefits evenly throughout the tax year under the PAYE system.

If:

- your tax code has two letters or no number; or

- is the letter D followed by a zero;

it is normally used where you have two or more sources of income and all of your allowances are in the tax code to be applied in working out the tax payable on the income from your main employment.

How tax is worked out using your tax code

The coding notice issued to Simon Black for 2011/12 tells him that his tax-free amount for the year is £1,350. He earns £32,760 per annum in his job.

The deduction for tax is worked out as follows:

	£
Pay from employment	32,760.00
Less: tax-free amount for year	1,350.00
Tax due on	£31,410.00

	£
Income Tax payable £31,410 @ 20%	6,228.00

To work out the weekly amounts of pay and tax, divide the pay and tax payable for the year by 52:

Weekly pay is £32,760 ÷ 52 = £630.00

Weekly tax is £6,228 ÷ 52 = £119.77

To work out the equivalent monthly amount divide by 12:

Monthly pay is £32,760 ÷ 12 = £2,730.00

Monthly tax is £6,228 ÷ 12 = £519.00

Form P60

Shortly after the end of each tax year every employer sends HMRC a Return summarizing:

- the names of all employees;

- their earnings during that tax year; and

- the deductions made for both Income Tax and National Insurance Contributions.

By 31 May following the end of a tax year your employer must give you your Form P60. This is a certificate of your earnings for the past tax year and it also lets you know how much Income Tax and National Insurance Contributions you have paid. Over the page is an illustration of the Form P60 sent to Simon Black by his employer for 2010/11. This shows:

- the tax deducted from his earnings in the year amounted to £5,120.00 based on a tax code of 92L;

- he incurred National Insurance contributions totalling £2,285.55.

Do not destroy **P60 End of Year Certificate** **2010–11**

Your employer's name and address

BROADWOOD ENGINEERS LTD
BRIDGE STREET
BROADWOOD
PT3 7GN

Tax Year to 5 April **2011**
HM Revenue & Customs office name

BROADWOOD

Employer PAYE reference
28 / B604

Employee's details

National Insurance number	BZ 62 24 17 A	

Gender **M** ◆ 'M' – male, 'F' – female

Surname **BLACK**

First two forenames **SIMON**

Your private address
12 CHURCH RISE
BROADWOOD
PT3 8ZL

Works/payroll number

National Insurance contributions 'in this employment' *(Note: LEL = Lower Earnings Limit, ET = Earnings Threshold UAP = Upper Accrual Point, UEL = Upper Earnings Limit)*

NICs table letter	Earnings at the LEL (where earnings are equal to or exceed the LEL) (whole £s)	Earnings above the LEL, up to and including the ET (whole £s)	Earnings above the ET, up to and including the UAP (whole £s)	Earnings above the UAP, up to and including the UEL (whole £s)		Employee's contributions due on all earnings above the ET		Scheme Contracted-out Number (For Contracted-out Money Purchase schemes OR Contracted-out Money Purchase Stakeholder Pension schemes only)
	£	£	£	£		£	p	
A	5044	671	20805			2285	55	S S S S

Statutory payments included in the pay 'In this employment' figure below

	£ p		£ p
		Statutory Maternity Pay (SMP)	

| Statutory Paternity Pay (SPP) | £ p | Statutory Adoption Pay (SAP) | £ p |

Student Loan deductions
In this employment (whole £s) £

Pay and Income Tax details

	Pay £ p	Tax deducted £ p	Enter 'R' in this box if net refund
In previous employment(s)			
In this employment ★	26520 00 ■	5120 00 ◀	
Total for year	26520 00	5120 00	

The figures aside marked ★ should be used for your tax return, if you get one

Employee's Widows and Orphans Life Assurance contributions in this employment ★ £ p

Final tax code **92L**   Week 53 payment indicator ◀

For employer's use

To the employee: keep this certificate in a safe place. You will need it if you fill in a tax return. You also need it to make a claim for tax credits or to renew your claim. It also helps you check that your employer is using the correct National Insurance number and deducting the right rate of National Insurance contributions. **By law you are required to tell HM Revenue & Customs about any income that is not fully taxed, even if you are not sent a tax return.**

HM REVENUE & CUSTOMS

Certificate by Employer/Paying Office:
This form shows your total pay for Income Tax purposes in this employment for the year. Any overtime, bonus, commission etc, Statutory Sick Pay, Statutory Maternity Pay, Statutory Paternity Pay or Statutory Adoption Pay is included.

P60(LaserSheet 3–Portrait)(2010–11)

Employer: For completion by desktop laser printer or other suitable sheet-feed printer. Forms P14 (National Insurance and Tax copies) are on separate sheets 1 and 2.

HMRC 10/09

Starting work

If you are starting a job for the first time, or have not already been in work during the tax year, your employer will ask you to fill in a Form P46 and to provide some other information. This will enable your employer to receive a tax code for you from HMRC so that the right deductions for Income Tax can be made from your wage or salary.

Moving jobs

Whenever you change your job your old employer hands you parts 1A, 2 and 3 of Form P45. On this form are your name and address, the name and address of your past employer, your tax district and reference number, and your code number at the date of leaving. It also includes your cumulative salary and the tax deductions for the tax year up to the date that you leave, and your salary and tax deductions from the last employment unless this information is the same as the cumulative figures. Your ex-employer sends the first part of the Form P45 to his tax district.

Parts 2 and 3 of the Form P45 must be given to your new employer. He enters your address and the date of starting your latest job before sending part 3 of the form to his own Tax Office. The information from the form allows your current employer to make the correct deductions for Income Tax and National Insurance from your new salary or wage right from the start of the new job.

You should keep Part 1A of the form for your own records, because it may be helpful when you come to prepare your own Tax Return.

If you do not have a P45 to give to your new employer, you will find that the deductions you incur for Income Tax are equivalent to those of an individual with just a personal allowance. This is known as the 'Emergency' code. Where this happens you should:

- either ask for, and complete a Tax Return; or

- send in sufficient information to your new employer's Tax Office so that the correct code number can be issued.

Tax-deductible expenses

The rules allowing you to claim tax relief on expenses connected with your employment are extremely restricted. You are denied tax relief on almost all types of expense which are not ultimately borne by your employer. This is because, as an employee, you have to show that any expenditure is incurred 'wholly, exclusively and necessarily' in performing the duties of your employment. If your employer will not foot the bill for the expenditure involved, then HMRC take the view that it was incurred as a matter of choice rather than of necessity. Nevertheless, some business expenses paid personally are deductible from your income and should be claimed on your Tax Return.

They include:

- annual subscriptions to a professional body;

- business use of your own car and telephone;

- clothing and upkeep of tools – HMRC and the Trade Unions have agreed flat-rate allowances for the upkeep of tools and special clothing in most classes of industry. The current rates are set out in Appendix 2. As an alternative you can claim a deduction for the actual amount spent on these items; and

- payment by directors or employers for work-related insurance cover. Tax relief is also allowed on meeting the cost of uninsured liabilities.

Tax-free expenses

The cost of most expenses you incur in your work is ultimately met by your employer, who either reimburses you on an expense claim or pays for them direct. Tax free for everyone are:

- luncheon vouchers up to 15p per day;

- free or subsidised meals in a staff canteen, providing the facilities can be used by all staff;

- sporting and recreational facilities;

- staff parties, providing the annual cost to the employer is no more then £150 per head;

- awards for long service of at least 20 years. The cost of the articles purchased by the employer must not exceed £50 for each year of service;

- gifts not exceeding £250 in the tax year to an employee from a third party by reason of his or her employment;

- one routine health check and one medical screening each year;

- eye tests and corrective glasses if your employer is required, by law, to provide eye and eyesight tests for you because of the work you do;

- work-related training expenses including fees, travel, reasonable subsistence and the cost of any books;

- the cost of out-placement counselling and retraining courses for both full- and part-time employees;

- equipment or facilities provided to disabled people to enable them to carry out their jobs;

- computer equipment loaned to employees before 6 April 2006 providing the cash equivalent of the benefit does not come to more than £500 annually. Any excess over £500 is taxable;

- one mobile telephone per employee for private use. But the exemption continues for multiple telephones provided to employees before 6 April 2006;

- childcare facilities at the workplace or elsewhere (but not on domestic premises);

- employer-supported childcare of up to £55 a week. Employers can either contract with an approved child carer or provide childcare vouchers;

- up to £3 per week paid to you by your employer for working at home as part of your employment contract. You are not required to produce any supporting evidence of the costs you incur;

- accommodation and subsistence expenses when your duties require you to travel abroad. HMRC has published a list of benchmarks for use by your employer. Only payments in excess of the rates are taxable;

- personal incidental expenses when you stay away from home overnight on business. The most common expenses covered are newspapers, telephone calls to home and laundry. The tax-free limits, including VAT, are £5 per night for stays anywhere in the UK and £10 per night elsewhere. Where these limits are exceeded the whole payment becomes payable – not the excess;

- bicycle and cycling safety equipment made available to employees mainly to get them between home and work;

- parking facilities for cars, motorcycles or bicycles at or near your place of work;

- a works' bus service;

- the cost of infrequent private transport when you have been working late and either public transport is no longer available or it would be unreasonable to expect you to use it at a late hour. Infrequent late working means working until at least 9.00 pm not more than 60 times in a tax year; and

- mileage allowances where employees use their car, van, motorcycle or pedal cycle on business. The tax-free rates laid down by HMRC for 2010/11 are:

  Cars and Vans

— First 10,000 miles	40p per mile
— Excess	25p per mile
Motorcycles	24p per mile
Bicycles	20p per mile

Employees are taxed on payments made by their employers over and above the rates in the table, but they can claim back on the difference where their employers pay them less than the permitted rate.

Employee travel

The cost of travelling between home and work is not allowable for tax purposes, other than for disabled employees who are given financial help by their employers with home-to-work travel on public transport or by some other means.

However, tax relief is allowed on all your business travel where your journey starts from either home or your permanent workplace. Where the full cost of a journey is not reimbursed by your employer, you can claim tax relief on the excess miles not paid for by your employer.

(a) Site-based workers

These are employees who work at a number of different places for periods of a few weeks or months at a time. Travelling expenses reimbursed to them are tax free providing:

- the worker initially expects the posting not to exceed two years, and the stay must actually last for less than this time;

- there is no requirement for an employee to return to his or her permanent workplace when each site job comes to an end; or

- an employee's work on site may be considered as a single continuous period even if he or she is occasionally moved off-site.

(b) Employees with areas

The geographical area covered by employees such as salesmen is treated as their permanent place of work. The following special rules apply:

- all travel within the area is eligible for tax relief;

- where an employee lives outside his or her area, travel to the start of the area is classified as home-to-work travel and is taxable if paid for by the employer; or

- the entire country is likely to be the area for any employee whose duties extend to servicing customers throughout the whole of the UK.

All travelling appointments of service engineers are treated as business travel qualifying for tax relief.

(c) More than one workplace

No tax relief is due for travel from home to either place of work for employees with more than one permanent place of location. It is HMRC's view that a workplace is likely to be considered as permanent if:

- an employee regularly performs 40% or more of the duties of the employment there;

- customers, suppliers and others would expect to make contact with the employee there; and

- the employee has an office, or desk, and support services.

Home working

A growing number of people are now giving up the daily commute in favour of working from home, either full-time or on a part-time basis. This is being made increasingly possible because of modern technology.

However, to get tax benefits, you must be able to demonstrate that you work from home as a necessity rather than by choice. If you satisfy this test you should be able to claim tax relief on:

- a proportion of your household costs such as heating, lighting, telephone and water (if any);

- use of your car, computer and tools for your employer's business; and

- other expenses you incur on stationery, books and professional subscriptions for the business.

Benefits-in-kind

Employees (including full-time working directors who own 5% or under of the company's shares) earning less than £8,500 per annum, including expenses, are not taxed on most benefits or perks provided by their employers. In addition to the list of tax-free expenses, the most valuable non-taxable benefits for this class of employee are private medical insurance and a company car.

Other directors and employees (including full-time working directors), whose total earnings, including expenses, exceed £8,500 per annum, are generally taxed on the actual value of any employment-related benefits and taxable expenses. Information about your expense payments and benefits-in-kind is supplied by your employer to your Tax Office each year on a Form P11D. Your employer should give you a copy of this form by 6 July following the end of the tax year. It sets out your employer's calculations of your taxable payments and cash equivalents of benefits-in-kind. It is up to you to claim those that are not taxable. This should not cause you any problem where expenses such as travelling and entertaining have genuinely arisen from the performance of the duties of your employment.

There are set rules for calculating some benefits.

(a) Company cars

The tax charge is based on a percentage of the list price of a car (subject to a ceiling of £80,000) but graduated according to the level of the car's carbon dioxide (CO_2) emissions. The minimum charge is 5% of list price, increasing to a maximum of 35% if CO_2 emissions are above the prescribed level.

In view of their higher emissions of pollutants diesel cars are subject to a 3% supplementary charge. However, even for diesel cars the maximum charge cannot exceed 35% of a car's price.

The car benefit charges for cars with an approved CO_2 emissions figure for the 2010/11 tax year are as follows:

CO_2 emissions in g/km	% of list price which is taxed	
	Petrol	*Diesel*
75 or less	5	8
120	10	13
130	15	18
135	16	19
140	17	20
145	18	21
150	19	22
155	20	23
160	21	24
165	22	25
170	23	26
175	24	27
180	25	28
185	26	29
190	27	30
195	28	31
200	29	32
205	30	33
210	31	34
215	32	35
220	33	35
225	34	35
230	35	35

There is a 2% discount from the appropriate percentage rate for cars manufactured to run on E85 fuel.

The regime extends to all cars, not just new ones. However, special rules apply to:

- older cars (those registered before 1 January 1998); and

- cars first registered on or after 1 January 1998 with no CO_2 emissions.

Cars first registered before 1 January 1998 will have no CO_2 emissions figures and, therefore, the taxable car benefit is worked out on a percentage of list price based on engine size:

Engine size	% of list price which is taxed
Up to 1,400	15
1,401–2,000	22
2,001 or more	32

The same applies to cars registered on or after 1 January 1998 with no CO_2 emissions figures, as follows:

Engine size	% of list price which is taxed
Up to 1,400	15 (18% if diesel)
1,401–2,000	25 (28% if diesel)
2,001 or more	35

Where a car has no cylinder capacity the percentage limit is 35%.

For a car which cannot produce CO_2 engine emissions, such as an electrically propelled car, there is no taxable benefit.

Mileage between home and work counts as private, not business, usage except in a car made available to an employee who:

- has a travelling appointment; or

- travels from home to a temporary place of work and the distance travelled is less than the distance between the normal place of work and the temporary place of work; or

- is a home worker and travels from home to another place of work in the performance of his or her duties.

There are several other circumstances where home-to-work travel in an employer-provided car is considered to be private use but is disregarded for tax purposes. These are where the car is provided:

- to a disabled person for home-to-work travel and there is no other private use;

- for home-to-work travel when public transport is disrupted; and

- for late-night journeys home from work.

(b) Fuel benefits

If your employer pays for fuel for your private motoring this also gives rise to a taxable benefit on which you have to pay Income Tax. The taxable amount is calculated on the car benefit percentage for the CO_2 emissions of your car multiplied by 18,000, giving the following taxable benefits for the 2010/11 tax year:

CO_2 emissions in g/km	% of list price which is taxed		Taxable benefit (£)	
	Petrol	*Diesel*	*Petrol*	*Diesel*
120	10	13	1,800	2,340
130	15	18	2,700	3,240
135	16	19	2,880	3,420
140	17	20	3,060	3,600
145	18	21	3,240	3,780
150	19	22	3,420	3,960
155	20	23	3,600	4,140
160	21	24	3,780	4,320
165	22	25	3,960	4,500
170	23	26	4,140	4,680
175	24	27	4,320	4,860
180	25	28	4,500	5,040
185	27	29	4,680	5,220
190	27	30	4,860	5,400
195	28	31	5,040	5,580
200	29	32	5,220	5,760
205	30	33	5,400	5,940
210	31	34	5,580	6,120
215	32	35	5,760	6,300
220	33	35	5,940	6,300
225	34	35	6,120	6,300
230	35	35	6,300	6,300

The benefit is:

- reduced to zero if the full cost of fuel for all your private motoring is reimbursed to your employer;

- proportionately reduced if you stop enjoying the use of free fuel for non-business motoring partway through a tax year; and

- not charged for any period of at least 30 days during which your car cannot be used or is unavailable to you.

(c) Company vans

If your employer provides you with a company van

- without any unrestricted use,

- no matter the age or size of the van,

you are taxed on a fixed amount of £3,000.

However, there is no taxable benefit:

- if the only personal use permitted by your employer is driving the van between your home and work; or

- your van is propelled solely by electricity.

There is an additional benefit of £550 where your employer pays for fuel for private mileage.

(d) Pooled vehicles

The private use of a car from an employer's pool of vehicles will not give rise to a tax charge on an employee provided:

- any home-to-work travel is merely incidental to business use; and

- the vehicle is not garaged at or near the employee's home overnight.

(e) Living accommodation

In some trades it is established practice for an employer to provide living accommodation. This can also be desirable where there is a security risk. No Income Tax liability arises in either set of circumstances.

In other situations Income Tax is chargeable on the annual value of the property after deducting any rent paid for it. For these purposes the annual valuation is broadly equivalent to the gross rateable value. Estimated rateable values will be used for new properties not appearing on the domestic rating list.

An additional tax charge arises where the accommodation costs more than £75,000. This is worked out by applying HMRC's official interest rate (see below) to the excess of the cost price above £75,000.

(f) Beneficial loans

The rules dealing with interest-free or low-rate-interest loans from an employer are as follows:

- the taxable benefit is worked out by applying HMRC's official rate of interest to the loan, currently 4.00%;

- any interest actually paid on the loan reduces the amount of the benefit;

- no tax charge arises where all of an employee's cheap or interest-free loans, excluding loans that qualify for tax relief, total less than £5,000;

- there is no tax charge where the loan is for a purpose on which the interest would qualify for tax relief (see Chapter 4).

(g) Medical insurance

You will be taxed on the cost of private medical insurance premiums paid by your employer for you or other members of your family. Not subject to tax is the cost of medical insurance cover, or actual medical treatment overseas, while away on business.

(h) Relocation expenses

An employee who changes his job, or is relocated by his employer, is not taxed on the costs of a relocation package up to £8,000. This limit applies to each job-related move. There are specific definitions for the removal expenses and benefits that qualify for exemption within the monetary limit.

Employee share ownership

There are a variety of share, profit sharing and share option schemes, all offering different investment limits and tax reliefs – some more generous than others.

(a) Under a Share Incentive Plan:

- employers can give employees up to £3,000 of shares free of Income Tax and National Insurance;

- some or all of these shares can be awarded to employees for reaching performance targets;

- employees are able to buy partnership shares out of their pre-tax salary or wage up to a maximum of 10% of salary or £1,500 a year, free of Income Tax and National Insurance;

- employers can match partnership shares by giving employees up to two free shares for each partnership share they buy;

- employees who sell their shares are liable to Capital Gains Tax only on any increase in the value of their shares after they come out of a plan;

- free and matching shares must normally be kept in the plan for at least three years – employees can take partnership shares out of the plan at any time;

- shares must come out of the plan when employees leave and some employees may lose their free and matching shares if they leave their jobs within three years of getting the shares;

- dividends, up to £1,500 annually, paid on the shares are tax free providing they are reinvested in additional shares in the company and retained for at least three years;

- employees who keep their shares in a plan for five years pay no Income Tax or National Insurance on those shares;

- employees who take their shares out of a plan after three years pay Income Tax and National Insurance on no more than the initial value of the shares – any increase in the value of their shares while in the plan is free of Income Tax and National Insurance; and

- Capital Gains Tax roll-over relief is available for existing shareholders of smaller companies who want to sell their shares to a new plan trust to be used for the benefit of employees.

(b) The main features of a Savings-Related Share Option Scheme are:

- it operates in combination with either a bank or building society SAYE savings contract under which employees save a fixed regular amount each month;

- the maximum amount that can be saved is £250 per month over either a three or five-year period;

- the price at which options can be offered to directors and employees cannot be less than 80% of the market value of the shares at the time the options are granted; and

- the receipt of the options and any increase in the value of the shares between the time that the options are granted and the date when they are exercised are free of Income Tax.

(c) Under an Approved Profit-Sharing Scheme:

- a company makes an allocation of profits to Trustees who, in turn, use the contribution in acquiring shares in the company which are subsequently allotted to employees;

- the limit on the market value of shares which may be appropriated to any one individual in each tax year is 10% of salary with a minimum limit of £3,000 and a maximum of £8,000; and

- there is no Income Tax liability when the shares are set aside or if they are retained by the Trustees of the scheme for three years.

(d) Inland Revenue Approved Share Option Plan:

- no liability to Income Tax is imposed on a director or employee who acquires, or disposes of, ordinary shares under such a plan;

- the market value of shares, at the time of the grant of the option, over which an individual holds unexercised rights under the plan must not exceed £30,000;

- an option must be exercised not less than three, or more than 10, years after it is granted, or under three years after a previous exercise;

- the gain is measured by the difference between the sale proceeds and the cost of acquiring the shares, and is charged to Capital Gains Tax at the time of disposal; and

- the price payable must be fixed at the time of the grant and must not be less than the market value of the shares at that date.

Enterprise Management Incentives

Enterprise Management Incentives are aimed at:

- helping small companies attract and retain the key people they need; and

- rewarding employees for taking a risk by investing their time and skills in helping small companies achieve their potential.

Normally, without any charge to Income Tax or National Insurance, companies can grant share options to employees worth up to £120,000 at the time of the grant.

A qualifying employee is one who must spend at least 25 hours a week, or if less, 75% of their working time on the business of that company.

Payments on termination of employment

It is often the practice for an employee to be paid a lump sum on the termination of an employment. If the right to receive the lump sum arose during the employment then it is taxable in full in the same way as any other earnings. Otherwise the lump sum payment is either wholly or partly tax free. Such payments are free of tax where:

- the employment ceases because of the accidental death, injury or disability of the employee; or

- most of the employee's time was spent working overseas for the employer.

Where the lump sum payment is made at a time other than on death or retirement, then the first £30,000 is tax free. It is only the excess of any payment over £30,000 that is taxable.

Any statutory redundancy repayment you receive, although it is itself exempt from tax, has to be added to any other lump sum payment from your employer in working out the Income Tax due on the amount.

It is not unusual for redundancy and employment termination settlements to provide for benefits, such as membership of a company medical insurance scheme, to continue after the employment has come to an end. Such payments and benefits are taxed only to the extent that they actually arise, and in the year in which they are received or enjoyed.

Belinda Morrison was made redundant in May 2010. Under her employment termination settlement she received lump sum payments of £26,000 and £20,000 on 19 May 2010 and 7 April 2011 respectively. She was also permitted to retain her membership of her employer's company medical insurance scheme for four years at an annual cost to her employer of £1,000. Belinda's total redundancy package for 2010/11 comes to £27,000. As this is below the £30,000 exemption limit she does not pay tax on any part of the package she received in 2010/11. The balance of the exemption limit of £3,000 is carried forward to 2011/12 to be set against the cash payment of £20,000 and the medical insurance benefit of £1,000. For 2011/12, therefore, Belinda's old employer will deduct tax on £18,000.

6   VALUE ADDED TAX

Value Added Tax (VAT) is a system for taxing what people spend. It is also administered by HMRC. The National Advice Service (NAS) is the main contact point for businesses. The NAS telephone number is 0845 010 9000.

What is VAT?

VAT is a self-assessed tax charged on:

- the supply of goods and services in the UK; and

- the import of goods and certain services into the UK.

It applies where a taxable person in business makes supplies which are taxable supplies.

Rates of VAT

There are three rates of VAT; a standard rate of 20.0% (which was increased from 17.5% on 4 January 2011), a reduced rate of 5% and a zero rate. Most of the goods and services supplied in the UK are liable to tax at the standard rate. Among the goods and services liable at the two lower rates are:

- Supplies charged at 5%:

    — domestic fuel and power

    — renovations and alterations of dwellings

    — residential conversions

- Zero-rated supplies:

    — food sold in shops

    — books and newspapers

    — children's clothing and footwear

    — construction of new houses

— passenger transport

— exports of goods.

Exempt supplies

Some goods and services have no VAT on them.

- Exempt supplies:
  - education
  - health and welfare
  - insurance
  - land
  - finance and banking transactions

If you sell goods or supply services which are exempt you do not charge VAT, but neither can you recover VAT charged on the purchases and expenses of your business. Special rules apply where your business makes both chargeable and exempt supplies.

Registration

If you are just starting up a business it is unlikely you will need to register for VAT immediately. Only when the value of your taxable supplies reaches £70,000 in a 'rolling' 12-month period is it compulsory to apply for registration. In working out the turnover of your business for this purpose remember that taxable supplies are not just those liable at the standard rate but include supplies liable to tax at the lower rates of 5% and zero.

Simon Potter started up in business in August 2009. He has been successful in building up his turnover each month. Looking back from the end of January 2011 his turnover for the previous twelve months was £68,000. But when he did the same exercise a month later this figure had increased to £72,000. Simon had to notify liability to register by 31 March 2011 and was registered for VAT from 1 April 2011.

You also need to register if the taxable supplies of your business are likely to exceed the registration limit of £70,000 in the next 30 days. Also, do not delay making an application for registration if you acquire an existing business where the previous owner was VAT registered. Sometimes it is possible for you to take on the same registration number as that of the previous owner.

You can only avoid registration if you can satisfy HMRC that either:

- your taxable turnover is expected to decline so that, from then on, it will remain at an annual level under £68,000; or

- your business activities are such that, if registration was in place, you would normally receive repayments of VAT.

Form VAT1 has to be used to register for VAT. You can normally expect to receive your VAT number within 15 working days. You can help the registration process by:

- applying for your registration in good time;

- ensuring that your application is complete and accurate; and

- sending your application to HM Revenue and Customs, Registration Unit, Deansgate, 62-70 Tettenhall Road, Wolverhampton WV1 4TZ.

Alternatively, you can apply to register by using the HMRC VAT Online Service.

Your formal certificate of registration will follow a week or two after you have received the letter advising you of your VAT number. You will probably also be sent one or two leaflets of a general nature. There may be other information which would be of benefit to you and your business. Appendix 3 at the end of the book lists some of the VAT notices currently available from the NAS.

Voluntary registration

Sometimes there are benefits from VAT registration even though the turnover of your business is below the compulsory limit for registration. Voluntary registration is allowed providing you can show that you are, or will be, making some taxable supplies.

An advantage of voluntary registration is that you can reduce your costs by recovering VAT incurred on your business expenses, including VAT paid on certain start-up costs and on the acquisition of assets such as computers and printers.

But if your customers are the general public, voluntary registration is not likely to be beneficial. They cannot recover the VAT charged on your goods and services so you may be putting yourself at a price disadvantage compared to your competitors.

Cancellation of registration

You can apply to HMRC to deregister your business from VAT:

- where the taxable turnover in the previous year was below the registration threshold of £70,000; or

- the anticipated turnover in the coming 12 months will be below £68,000.

Deregistration is compulsory where:

- you cease to trade; or

- you sell your business.

Help from HMRC

It is the policy of HMRC to try and make contact with new businesses soon after they have become registered so that:

- any queries which may already have arisen can be resolved;

- you can be offered videos on various aspects of the tax, an opportunity to attend a seminar or, alternatively, a one-to-one meeting to discuss matters of a more individual nature; and

- the advantages of the simplification measures available to smaller businesses can be pointed out to you.

It is unusual these days for HMRC to take a hard-line approach when smaller businesses, new to VAT, run into difficulties in preparing their first one or two VAT Returns or paying the tax shown to be due. Any initial difficulties are, however, expected to be only short-term.

If you have an enquiry of a technical nature I suggest you set out the details in a letter to HMRC. The NAS will let you have the address of the office to which you should write.

VAT invoices

There are a number of items which you must show on all VAT invoices issued by your business. These mandatory requirements are:

- the date of issue;
- a sequential number which uniquely identifies the invoice;
- your VAT identification number;
- the full name and address of both your own business and that of your customer;
- a description of the quantity and nature of the goods supplied or services rendered;
- the time of the supply;
- the net unit price;
- the gross amount payable, excluding VAT;
- the rate of VAT charged; and
- the amount of VAT payable.

There are also other specific requirements but these only apply in certain circumstances such as supplies to and from other EU countries.

You are also allowed to issue invoices electronically. Furthermore you can agree with your customers that they will raise the invoices for the goods or services you have supplied to them. This practice is known as self-billing.

Records, accounting and returns

If your business is VAT registered you must:

- render tax invoices for all taxable supplies of goods and services;
- maintain an account showing the calculations of your VAT liability for each VAT period; and
- make timely VAT Returns to HMRC.

The VAT payable, or repayable, each period is the simple difference between your VAT output tax and input tax. Output tax is what you charge on the goods and services (outputs) to your customers. Input tax is what you incur on the purchases and expenses (inputs) of running your business. You should keep copies of every invoice for all your sales and purchases which should be filed in an orderly manner.

Totalling the VAT on your outputs and inputs each month should make it fairly straightforward to bring together the information you need to complete the VAT Return – Form VAT100 – for the accounting periods shown on your registration certificate.

Beth Way runs a hairdressing salon which is VAT registered. She has been given quarterly VAT accounting periods in line with the calendar quarters. She accounts for VAT as a retailer on the basis of the income received each quarter. Her VAT account for the three months to the end of March 2011 was:

	£	£
Output Tax		
January	1,940	
February	1,830	
March	2,070	
Total	£5,840	5,840
Input Tax		
January	220	
February	160	
March	250	
Total	£630	630
Net amount due to HMRC		£5,210

The various boxes on your VAT Return can be filled in from the figures in your VAT account and the tax-exclusive values of your outputs and inputs for the period.

Make sure you submit each Return and pay what is due to HMRC within the stipulated time limit. If the VAT you have reclaimed on the purchases and expenses of the business exceeds the VAT on your turnover for the period, the Return will show you are entitled to a repayment which will be sent direct to your bank account.

If you wish, you can request that your quarterly VAT Return periods coincide with your financial year.

All VAT Returns and payments should now be sent to the VAT Controller, VAT Central Unit, BX5 5AT.

Payments are treated as received when cleared funds reach HMRC's bank account. If you pay by cheque you must allow sufficient time for your payment to:

- reach HMRC; and

- clear by no later than the due date shown on your paper VAT Return.

Online filing of Returns

If your business:

- has a VAT exclusive turnover of at least £100,000; or

- registered for VAT on or after 1 April 2010 you must file your VAT Returns online and pay any VAT due electronically.

There are a number of benefits from online filing such as up to an extra seven days to

- file your return; and

- pay any VAT due.

To pay by the internet, telephone or BACS Credit Card you need the following information:

Sort code: 08-32-00
Account number: 11963155
Account Name: HMRC VAT

Quote your VAT registration number leaving no gaps.

When signing up for online filing you should:

- provide an email address; and

- set up an email reminder. This will be the only communication to you from HMRC that it is now time to complete a Return.

Input tax

The actual amount of input tax on purchases does not matter quite so much when the Flat Rate Scheme is used; see page 66. For other businesses it is only the input tax on the costs of the business which can be claimed when VAT Returns are completed. Sometimes expenses may be incurred where input tax cannot be claimed at all. Examples are business entertaining and private purchases paid for through your business. Occasionally there may be a need to apportion input tax, such as that on home telephone bills which are partly for business and partly for private purposes. Apportionment is best done on a percentage basis which, provided it is reasonable, HMRC can be expected to accept.

Motor cars and fuel

Businesses directly concerned with motoring, like new car dealers, vehicle hirers, taxi drivers or driving schools, may be able to reclaim all input tax on cars which they buy or lease. Input tax cannot be claimed back on cars bought by other businesses and made available for private use. However, it may be possible to claim 50% of the input tax on the rental payments where cars are leased.

There are two alternative methods for dealing with input tax on motor fuel, namely:

- all input tax is claimed and a fixed-scale charge to take account of private use is applied. From 1 May 2010 the fuel scale charges, based on a 20.0% rate, for a three-month period are as follows:

CO_2 emissions in g/km	Scale charge £	VAT due £
120 and below	141	23.50
121-135	212	35.33
136-139	227	37.83
140-144	241	40.16
145-149	255	42.50
150-154	269	44.83
155-159	283	47.16
160-164	297	49.50
165-169	312	52.00
170-174	326	54.33
175-179	340	56.66
180-184	354	59.00
185-189	368	61.33
190-194	383	63.83
195-199	397	66.16
200-204	411	68.50
205-209	425	70.83
210-214	439	73.16
215-219	454	75.66
220-224	468	78.00
225-229	482	80.33
230 and above	496	82.60

- no input tax is claimed and the fixed-scale charge is ignored. If you intend to deal with motor fuel this way you should write to HMRC to tell them.

Input tax on repairs and maintenance of business cars can be claimed whichever way you decide to deal with motor fuel.

Bad debts

Late or non-payment of bills can often have a serious impact on both the cash flow and profitability of a business. When it comes to bad debts it is only when a debt is more than six months old that an adjustment can be made to recover VAT accounted for on that debt in a previous VAT Return.

Adjustments for bad debts, although not separately shown on VAT Returns, must be recorded separately in the VAT account of your business. Listings must be maintained both to support the entries and any further adjustments made to reflect subsequent amounts recovered.

Special schemes for retailers

Retailers often sell a mixture of both positive and zero-rated goods but do not know how much of each of them is sold from day to day. When this happens they can use one of the schemes available to help them work out their VAT liabilities. If you are in retailing you should study the leaflets telling you about the various schemes so that you do not pay too much tax.

Where retailers only sell goods which are liable at the standard rate of 20.0%, the amount of tax included in the gross takings for a period is $1/6$. Referred to as the 'VAT fraction' this calculation is worked out as follows:

	£
Tax-exclusive value (say)	100.00
Add: VAT @ 20.0%	20.00
Tax-inclusive price	£120.00

The VAT included in the tax-inclusive price is therefore:

$$\frac{20.0}{120.0} = \frac{1}{6}$$

For goods liable at the reduced rate of 5% the 'VAT fraction' is $1/21$.

Where a retailer makes a supply for more than £250 the business must issue a proper tax invoice when asked to do so. For supplies under £250 there is usually enough information on till receipts for the 'VAT fraction' to be worked out by customers who, in the course of their business, make retail purchases and want to claim back the input tax suffered.

Flat Rate Scheme

The scheme is open to small businesses whose annual taxable turnover (not including VAT) does not exceed £150,000. It will be of particular appeal to businesses which do not want to spend too much time and effort dealing with all the administrative complications of normal VAT accounting. Under the scheme, VAT is still charged to customers at the rate appropriate to the supplies made by the business. When you come to complete your VAT Returns:

- you do not make a separate claim to recover input tax on purchases, expenses or low-value assets acquired for your business;

- any input tax on capital assets with a value of more than £2,000 may be claimable separately; and

- you work out the tax due by applying a fixed percentage to the VAT inclusive turnover of your business for the period.

The percentages have been set by HMRC according to the principal activity of a business and take into account that input tax on normal purchases is not claimed.

> Yvonne Spencer is a photographer. Her VAT inclusive turnover for the quarter to the end of March 2011 was £18,000. Yvonne must pay VAT of £1,980 as follows:
>
> £18,000 x 11% = £1,980

Businesses are being strongly encouraged by HMRC to use the scheme, so much so that a 1% reduction in the percentages for the first year is available to new businesses:

- that register for VAT when they should; and

- apply to use the scheme at the same time.

You have to leave the scheme once the regular annual turnover of your business reaches £230,000.

Cash accounting

Under the cash accounting scheme:

- you account for VAT on your outputs when you are paid for sales made by your business, rather than by reference to the date of your tax invoices; and

- you reclaim the VAT on your purchases and business expenses when you pay for them.

Your business is eligible to use this scheme from the beginning of a VAT tax period if:

- you expect the value of your taxable supplies (excluding VAT) during the forthcoming year to be no more than £1.35 million; and

- you are not in arrears in submitting past VAT Returns at the time you decide to join the scheme.

You must come out of cash accounting if:

- the amount of your taxable supplies exceeds £1.6 million (exclusive of VAT) in a period of one year; or

- your business fails to comply with the correct requirements for record keeping.

Annual accounting

Under the annual accounting scheme your business:

- submits just one VAT Return each year;

- makes interim payments of VAT based on an estimate of your liability for the year; and

- completes and sends in its VAT Return two months after the end of the year. At the same time you pay over the balance of VAT due.

You can apply to use the scheme if you reasonably believe that the amount of your taxable supplies, excluding VAT, in the period of twelve months from the date of your application will not exceed £1.35 million. If you are accepted on to the scheme the start date for the new arrangements will be the first day of your current accounting period. You will be notified in writing if your application has been accepted. The letter you receive will also tell you:

- the amount and timing of your interim payments; and

- the due date of the Annual Return and balancing payment.

Vince Charles is in business as a vehicle repairer and is registered for VAT. In October 2010 he applies to use the annual accounting scheme. His quarterly period runs from 1 September to 30 November. His first annual accounting period starts on 1 September 2010 and ends on 31 August 2011.

Once you are in the scheme you can remain in it until your annual turnover exceeds £1.6 million. You will then be taken off the scheme at the end of your current accounting year. Alternatively, if you want to come out of the scheme and go back to the normal method of paying and accounting for VAT you just need to tell HMRC of your decision.

Penalties, surcharges and interest

The penalty regime covering VAT aspects of your business extends to:

- failing to register for VAT on time; and

- errors in documents or Returns.

Penalties are calculated:

- as a percentage of the additional tax due;

- when the inaccuracy is put right.

The penalty is a percentage of the extra tax due and depends on the reason for the inaccuracy as follows:

Reason	Rate of Penalty	
	Maximum	**Minimum**
Reasonable Care	No penalty	
Carelessness	30%	0%
Deliberate	70%	20%
Deliberate and concealed	100%	30%

As you can see there is a substantial difference between the minimum and maximum rates of penalty. Therefore, even if you have adjusted for any error on the next VAT return after it was identified you should also:

- disclose the error with full details by writing to HMRC; and

- before it is picked up by HMRC itself;

- help HMRC calculate the extra VAT due; and

- allow HMRC to look at any records requested to check on the accuracy of the figures.

By doing all of this you should be able to secure a much reduced level of penalty.

Where a disclosure is made following a prompt from HMRC then the minimum levels of penalty are increased as follows:

	Rate
Carelessness	15%
Deliberate	35%
Deliberate and concealed	50%

Furthermore:

- default interest, at a rate broadly in line with commercial rates of interest, will normally be charged when assessments for errors are issued; and

- surcharges can be imposed by HMRC where you fail to:

    — file your VAT Returns on time; and/or

    — pay the proper amount of tax when it is due.

Default surcharges range from 2% to 15% where a history of default has built up. There is a minimum surcharge of £30. Surcharge assessments, at the 2% and 5% rates are, however, seldom issued unless they are calculated to exceed £400.

HMRC will pay you interest in cases where they make an official error but this is currently at the rate of 0.5%.

Appeals

You have the right to appeal to an Independent Tribunal against:

- the imposition of a penalty;

- the amount of a penalty; and

- a decision not to suspend a penalty.

Alternatively you can opt for an internal review by an independent HMRC officer. This is a quick and inexpensive way to resolve any dispute.

Complaints

VAT officers are committed to the same standards as Tax staff, see the Service Commitment reproduced in Chapter 1, and are expected to abide by them. If you ever feel dissatisfied with the manner in which the affairs of your business have been handled, or that an officer has overstepped the mark and has exceeded his authority, you can write to:

- the person who is in overall charge at the HMRC office for your business; or

- the Complaints Unit for the area where your business is situated.

If you are unable to resolve your complaint satisfactorily your next step is to contact the Adjudicator's Office, which is the independent body set up specifically for this purpose.

7 WORKING FOR YOURSELF

If you run your own business, other than through a company or in partnership, you are classified as self-employed for tax purposes. Your business might be a trade, profession or vocation.

Am I self-employed?

The main distinguishing factor between having self-employed status and working as an employee is the existence of a 'master–servant' relationship. Sometimes it is difficult to draw a line between:

- employment (a contract for service); and
- self-employment (a contract for services).

Your business will have the trappings of self-employment if you:

- are paid a fixed fee, rather than by the hour;
- have no entitlement to paid holidays or sick leave;
- are responsible for any losses arising out of your services or the goods you supply;
- can decide how, when and where the work should be undertaken;
- can dictate the hours you work; and
- provide your own tools.

You do not have to formalize any business relationship by entering into a contract for the supply of goods or services. Nevertheless, having a contract makes sound business sense because it will include matters other than those just relative to the taxation consequences of the relationship.

Starting up in business

Your business is now up and running. It is important that you quickly learn what you need to do about Tax, National Insurance (see Chapter 8) and maybe Value Added Tax (see Chapter 6). The best starting point is to telephone HMRC on 08459 15 45 15 and ask for a copy of their booklet 'Working for yourself – The Guide'. Reading it will help you understand what you need to know about keeping proper records of all your business transactions. It also covers other matters relevant to the self-employed taxpayer.

With the booklet comes Form CWF1 which you must complete to register for Tax and National Insurance.

Records

I strongly recommend that you maintain a separate bank account for all your business income, purchases and expenses. As a minimum you should keep the following books of account, either electronically or manually:

- a cash book to record and analyse your sales and other receipts, purchases and overhead expenses which pass through your bank account; and

- a petty cash book to log all small transactions paid for in cash.

If you run a larger business you will probably need to keep other accounting records as well. Whatever the size of your business it is a good discipline to write up all your books of account on a regular basis.

Furthermore, in order that you comply with the requirements for Self-Assessment, you should keep and file the following:

- invoices for sales made by your business;

- bank statements and paying-in slips to show where the income comes from;

- invoices for goods acquired or costs incurred;

- documentation supporting purchases and sales of assets used in your business; and

- records in support of amounts taken out of the business for personal use (drawings) and all money paid into your business from personal funds (capital introduced).

Accounts

You can choose the date to which you draw up the accounts of your self-employment each year. For this reason it is unlikely that the first accounts will cover a full year of the activities of your business. You can make up your accounts from the date you start in business to the end of:

- a particular month;

- your first year's trading;

- the calendar year on 31 December; or

- the tax year on 5 April.

Thereafter you should continue to draw up your accounts to the same date every year. You are allowed to change this date where you can show good reason to do so.

Your accounts should be drawn up to:

- work out the profit earned or loss sustained in the financial period; and

- summarize, whenever possible, on the balance sheet the amounts of the assets and liabilities at the year-end.

The statement of the profit or loss of your business is not usually the simple difference between receipts and payments. For example, if you sell to customers on credit there will inevitably be some unpaid sales at the year-end. These outstanding invoices need to come into your accounts as income for that period. Equally, where amounts are due to your suppliers for purchases or expenses at the end of your financial period these need to be included in the accounts as costs incurred in the period. If your business is:

- One which requires you to keep a stock of raw materials or finished goods, the value of that stock at the year-end must be included in the profit and loss statement as income. The basis of valuation is cost or, in the case of redundant or old stock, realizable value. The amount of your stock at the beginning of the accounting period is deductible as a cost.

- Of a professional nature or you are a service provider you must also make an adjustment to your accounts at the end of each accounting period. You must bring in as income an amount in respect of ongoing, but unbilled, work by reference to the proportion of the work completed.

When it comes to expenses make sure you claim all the overhead costs. For example:

- If you are married or live with a partner and your spouse/partner helps you in the business by doing your accounts and acting as a part-time secretary or assistant you can claim the salary paid to him/her as a business expense. You should pay a proper amount for these services. If this is his or her only job or income and the wage is less than £5,715 for the year then there will be no tax or National Insurance to pay.

- If you work from home you can claim a deduction for an appropriate proportion of the fixed costs of running your home, such as:

  — mortgage interest

  — council tax

  — light, heat and household insurance

  — the rental of your landline telephone

  — general repairs and maintenance

  — cleaning expenses

In order to be eligible you must have a specific area in your home set aside as an office.

There will be some costs of your business, such as a car used both privately and for work, when it may be difficult to apportion the expenditure between the private and business elements. Where there is this overlap, I suggest you include a note in the additional information section of the self-employed pages of your Tax Return, so your Tax Office can see how you have worked out the percentage of the expenditure chargeable to the business.

Dennis Cole started his business of supplying and fitting carpets back in August 2004. He has a shop in his local high street which he rents. His wife keeps his accounts, prepares his VAT Returns and helps part-time in the shop.

Dennis makes up his accounts to 31 July each year. The statement of his business income and expenses for the financial year to 31 July 2010 is as follows:

	£	£	£
Sales			340,540
Less: Cost of sales			
Stock of carpets and other materials at start of year		28,100	
Purchases during the year		179,100	
		207,200	
Less: Stock of carpets and other materials at end of year		31,350	175,850
Gross Profit			164,690
Less: Overhead expenses			
Wages of shop assistants and fitters		62,860	
Shop expenses			
Rent	15,000		
Business and water rates	3,340		
Light and heat	2,965		
Cleaning	2,100		
Insurance	1,640		
Window repairs	385		
		25,430	
Wife's salary		4,500	
Printing, postage and stationery		3,630	
Shop telephone and fax		1,380	
Advertising and promotion		5,220	
Van expenses		4,070	
Entertaining	240		
Accountancy		2,200	
Legal Fees – new lease		1,100	
Car expenses			
Road Fund Licence and Insurance	560		
Petrol and oil	1,410		
Repairs and servicing	620	2,590	
Use of home as office	($1/7$ x £2,450)	350	
Home telephone	(25%)	280	

Bank interest and charges	2,403	
Staff welfare	630	
Miscellaneous expenses	860	
	-------	117,743
Profit for the year		**£46,947**

Nowadays, annual accounts of a business are often needed for reasons other than tax. For example:

- to verify income in support of an application for a mortgage; or
- by your bank manager when weighting up an application for a business loan or overdraft facility.

Tax Return information

If you were in business at any time during the 2010/11 tax year you will need to complete the supplementary self-employment pages to accompany your Tax Return for the year. The self-employment pages are in a set format for reporting the annual income and expenses of your business. Your Return will not be accepted as complete if the information about your business income and expenses is not presented in the required format.

When Dennis Cole comes to complete the supplementary self-employment pages for the year ended 5 April 2011 he will fill in the section on business income and expenses, based on his accounts for the financial year to 31 July 2010, as follows:

	£
Sales/business income (excluding VAT)	340,540
Total Expenses	
Cost of goods bought for re-sale or goods used	175,850
Payments to subcontractors	—
Wages, salaries and other staff costs	67,360
Car, van and travel expenses	6,660
Rent, rates, power and insurance costs	23,295
Repairs and renewals of property and equipment	385
Telephone, fax, stationery and other office costs	7,390
Advertising and business entertainment costs	5,460

	£
Interest on bank and other loan, bank, credit card and other financial charges	2,403
Irrecoverable debts written off	—
Accountancy, legal and other professional fees	3,300
Other finance charges	—
Depreciation and loss/(profit) on sale of assets	—
Other business expenses	1,490
Total expenses	**£293,593**
Net profit	**£46,947**

Notes:

(1) Wages, salaries and other staff costs are:

Wages	62,860
Wife's salary	4,500
	£67,360

(2) Car, van and travel expenses are:

Van expenses	4,070
Car expenses	2,590
	£6,660

(3) Rent rates, power and insurance costs are:

Shop expenses (excluding cleaning and window repairs)	22,945
Use of home as office	350
	£23,295

(4) Telephone, fax, stationery and other office costs are:

Printing, postage and stationery	3,630
Telephone (shop and home)	1,660
Shop cleaning	2,100
	£7,390

(5) Advertising and business entertainment costs are: £

    Advertising and promotion   5,220

    Entertaining   240

        £5,460

(6) Accountancy, legal and other professional costs are:

    Accountancy   2,200

    Legal fees   1,100

        £3,300

So as to minimize the risk of HMRC raising enquiries into your self-employment income and Tax Return, you should adopt a consistent pattern from year-to-year in the way you analyse your business expenses under the various headings of the standardized format.

If the annual turnover of your business was below £70,000:

- you only need to complete the self-employment (short) supplementary pages; and

- you can add up all your business expenses allowable for tax purposes and just enter the total figure in box 19 on page SES1.

Profits for tax

The profit disclosed by your business accounts will not necessarily be the same as that on which your tax bill is calculated. This is because certain types of expenditure are specifically not allowable in working out taxable business profits. These include:

- the private proportion of mixed expenses;

- business entertainment;

- non-business charitable donations;

- amounts spent on items of a capital nature;

- professional costs related to capital expenditure; and

- general provisions and reserves.

Although Dennis Cole's accounts for his financial year to 31 July 2010 show he made a profit of £46,947, his taxable profit is £50,100 as follows:

	£	£
Profit as per accounts		46,947
Add: Disallowable expenses		
Private proportion of car expenses (70%)	1,813	
Entertainment	240	
Legal fees re new lease	1,100	
		3,153
Profit as adjusted for tax purposes		£50,100

Profits of the tax year

Self-employed individuals are taxed on the profits of their financial year ending in the tax year. This is known as 'the basis period'.

The tax-adjusted profit of £50,100 for the year to 31 July 2010 of Dennis Cole's carpet business will be taxed in 2010/11.

There are special rules for working out the profits on which you pay tax in the opening years of your business, as follows:

• in the first tax year your taxable profits are those arising in the period from commencement to the following 5 April;

• if you choose to prepare your business accounts up to a date 12 months after you began your business then, in the second tax year, you pay tax on the profits for the first full year of trading; and

• for the third and all subsequent tax years you pay tax on the profits for 'the basis period'.

Under these rules it is usual for the profits for some periods of account to be taken into account more than once in working out the amount on which you pay tax. However, over the lifetime of your business it is intended that the profits should be taxed in full but once and once only. As a result, profits which are taxed more than once are eligible for a special relief. Known as overlap relief it will be given when either:

- a business ceases; or
- for any earlier tax year where the basis period exceeds 12 months.

James Gray started up in business on 1 May 2010. His annual accounting date is 30 April. He makes the following profits in the first two years:

Year to 30.04.2011	£24,720
Year to 30.04.2012	£28,360

The taxable profits for the first three tax years are:

Tax Year	Basis Period	Taxable Profit
		£
2010/11	01.05.2010 to 05.04.2011	22,660
2011/12	Year to 30.04.2011	24,720
2012/13	Year to 30.04.2012	28,360

On cessation the taxable profits for the final tax year will be:

- those earned in the period from the end of the basis period in the previous tax year up to cessation, but reduced by:
- overlap relief.

James Gray decides to close down his business on 30 April 2018. In the final year James makes profits of £34,950. The final tax year is 2018/19 and James will pay tax on:

		£
Taxable profit of final year		34,950
Less: Overlap	01.05.2010 to 05.04.2011	22,660

Net taxable amount		£12,290
		======

Special rules apply when a business changes its accounting date. Apart from the first and last years of business the profits of a 12-month period are taxed in each tax year.

Sheila Windows began her business on 1 December 2010. She draws up her first accounts to 30 November 2011 and makes a profit of £33,000. She then decides to change her accounting date by extending it to 31 January 2013. The accounts for this 14-month period show a taxable profit of £28,000. Her basis period and taxable profits for the opening years of the business are:

Tax Year	Basis Period	Taxable Profit
		£
2010/11	01.12.2010 to 05.04.2011	11,000
2011/12	Year to 30.11.2011	33,000

The overlap period is from 01.12.2010 to 05.04.2011:

2012/13	01.12.2011 to 31.01.2013	
	(14 months)	28,000
Less: Overlap	01.12.2010 to 31.01.2011	5,500
		────────
Net taxable amount		£22,500
		────────

The overlap period was one of four months. As the accounting period from 1 December 2011 to 31 January 2013 is 14 months, the overlap is a period of two months. The amount deducted from the taxable profits for 2012/13 is half of the original overlap profit. A further two months of overlap relief is available either when the business ceases or in any subsequent tax year when the basis period is again longer than 12 months.

Post-cessation expenses

Tax relief is allowed on certain expenditure incurred after a business has ceased. The expenses which qualify for relief are those closely related to the trading or professional activities previously carried on but including, for example, relief for debts which have subsequently proved to be irrecoverable.

Relief is available for payments made within seven years of the permanent discontinuance of the business by setting the payments made against income for the same tax year. Any excess can be treated as a capital loss, but only of the same tax year.

Capital allowances

You can claim what are known as capital allowances on the expenditure you incur on items of a capital nature for your business.

Amounts spent by small businesses (your business is almost certain to qualify) attract the following rates of allowance in the first year:

- 100% on annual expenditure up to £100,000 on most types of plant and machinery;

- 100% on energy saving or environmentally beneficial plant and machinery;

- 100% for purchases of new low-emission cars for use by you or your staff in your business. To qualify a car must not emit more than 110 gm/km CO_2 or be electrically propelled;

- 100% on the purchase of new electric vans; and

- 20% for cars with CO_2 emissions of 160g/km or less. This rate reduces to 10% for cars exceeding this CO_2 emission limit.

In subsequent years your capital expenditure, after deducting your first year allowances, is further written down on the reducing-balance basis at the rate of 20% p.a. This rate is only 10% p.a. for cars purchased from 6 April 2009 onwards and with CO_2 emissions exceeding 160g/km. Where the unrelieved expenditure is no more than £1,000 you can claim tax relief on the full amount.

A separate 'pool' must be maintained for expenditure in each of the following different categories:

- all plant and equipment, including motor vans, lorries and cars with CO_2 emissions of 160g/km or less;

- all cars with CO_2 emissions exceeding 160g/km;

- each car bought before 6 April 2009 for over £12,000. The maximum writing down allowance is restricted to £3,000 for each car;

- each asset where there is both business and personal use; and

- each asset with a short life expectancy.

Where an asset on which capital allowances have been claimed is sold, you must bring the proceeds of sale into the computation of capital allowances. If it is sold:

- for less than the value to which it has been written-down for tax purposes you will probably be entitled to a further allowance equivalent to the difference between the sale proceeds and the written-down value.

These adjustments are respectively known as balancing allowances and balancing charges.

In his accounting year to 31 July 2010 Dennis Cole traded in his old car for £3,600 and bought a new one for £19,000 with a CO_2 emission limit of 160g/km. In the year he also spent £12,000 on a second-hand van, £1,500 on a computer and printer and £200 on a new filing cabinet. All these purchases were made after 6 April 2010. His claim to capital allowances for 2010/11, based on his capital expenditure in this year, is:

		Pool	Car with Private Use
	£	£	£
Written-down values brought forward from 2009/10		6,300	4,100
Sale proceeds of car			3,600
Balancing allowance			500
Additions in the year:			
Van, computer and cabinet		13,700	
New car			19,000
		20,000	
Allowances due:			
Annual Investment – 100%	13,700		
Writing down – 20%	1,260	14,960	3,800
Carried forward to 2011/12		£5,040	£15,200
Summary of allowances:			
Annual Investment		13,700	
Writing down		5,060	
Balancing		500	
		19,260	
Less: 70% private use of car		3,010	
2010/11 Capital allowances		£16,250	

Capital allowances are deducted from your profits as a trading expense of your business. Any balancing charges are treated as an addition to your profit. It follows that:

- the chargeable period for the purposes of working out your capital allowances is the same as that for which you draw up your accounts; and

- the length of the period of account determines the amount of writing-down allowances to which you are entitled.

Thus, if a period of account:

- is only nine months long, 9/12th of the writing-down allowances can be deducted from taxable profits for that period; or

- extends to 15 months, the tax deductible allowances equal 15/12th of the writing-down allowances.

Should a period of account exceed 18 months it must be divided into one of 12 months and a balancing period with restricted writing-down allowances.

There is a section in the supplementary self-employment pages in which you must summarize your claim to capital allowances.

Losses

It is almost inevitable that your business will go through both good and bad times. If you incur a loss you can claim tax relief on the loss sustained as increased by the amount of your capital allowances for the same period. You can choose whether to set a trading loss against other income in either the same, or the preceding, tax year. But you cannot claim to relieve only part of a loss.

Isabel Fletcher has been in business for many years. She makes up her accounts to 31 August each year. In the year ended 31 August 2011 she makes a loss which she can claim against her other income in 2011/12. Alternatively, the loss can be carried back and relieved against her total income in 2010/11.

Any unrelieved loss of your business then has to be carried forward for offset against profits from the same business in future years.

Alternatively you can claim to set a trading loss against capital gains (see Chapter 13) in the following way:

- the claim is for relief on the amount of the trading loss which cannot be set against your other income in the year or on which tax relief has already been given in some other way;

- the maximum loss eligible for relief against capital gains is the same as the amount of your gains chargeable to Capital Gains Tax; and

- it is not possible to make a partial claim.

By relieving a business loss this way you may be wasting personal allowances as well as your annual exemption for Capital Gains Tax.

Tax relief for losses incurred by new businesses is extended such that:

- Losses incurred during the first four tax years can be set against your total income for the three years prior to that in which the loss arises.

- Relief is first of all given against total income for the earliest year. For example, if you set up in business during 2010/11 and sustained a loss in the first period of trading, that part of the loss attributable to the 2010/11 tax year can be set against your income in 2007/08, 2008/09 and 2009/10, beginning with 2007/08.

Sometimes you may have to spend monies on a new business venture before you actually start to trade. Any such expenditure incurred within seven years before trading begins is treated as a separate loss of the tax year in which trading commences.

There is one final type of loss relief which is only available to those businesses which incur a loss in their last period of trading. In such circumstances there cannot be future profits against which such a loss might be relieved. Therefore, a loss arising in the last 12 months of trading can be set back against the profits from the same business in both the final and three preceding tax years, beginning with the profits of the last year and working backwards.

Ralph Collins retires from business on 30 September 2011. In the final nine months in business he loses £18,000. Previously his business had always been successful as follows:

Accounting Year		Taxable Profits £	Year of Charge
Year ended 31 December	2007	16,000	2007/08
Year ended 31 December	2008	12,000	2008/09
Year ended 31 December	2009	9,000	2009/10
Year ended 31 December	2010	4,000	2010/11

The terminal loss can be set off as follows:

2010/11	4,000	leaving nil taxable profits
2009/10	9,000	leaving nil taxable profits
2008/09	5,000	reducing the taxable profits to £7,000
	———	
	£18,000	

Taking on staff

You have now reached the time where your business is expanding. You need an assistant or an extra pair of hands. At this stage get in contact with the Tax Office dealing with your business. The information you give will be sent to the right department since it is likely to be a different office to that dealing with your business. You should be sent a New Employer's Starter Pack containing all the instructions, tables and forms you need.

As an employer you are responsible for:

- working out the deductions for Income Tax (PAYE) and National Insurance contributions from the salary or wage paid to your employees at regular weekly or monthly intervals;

- paying over the deductions to the Collector of Taxes each month. These payments can be made every quarter where your average monthly payments of PAYE and National Insurance contributions are less than £1,500;

- letting your Tax Office know every year how much each employee has earned together with the deductions made for both Income Tax and National Insurance contributions. The deductions should reconcile to the total of the amounts paid over to the Collector of Taxes. You must also give details of any benefits paid or provided; and

- giving your employees certificates showing their earnings for the tax year, deductions for Income Tax and National Insurance contributions and the value of any benefits provided.

Foster carers

Those who:

- receive income from local authorities or independent fostering providers for providing foster care to children and young people; or

- are qualified shared lives carers are entitled to a special relief which comes in two parts:

  — an exemption from Income Tax on receipts which do not exceed the qualifying amount for any year; and

  — a simplified optional method of calculating taxable profits where receipts are more than the qualifying amount.

The annual qualifying amount is made up of two parts which must be added together. They are:

- a fixed amount for each household – £10,000 for 2010/11; and

- a weekly amount for each foster child placed with you – for 2010/11, £200 a week for a child under age 11 and £250 a week for a child over 11 years old.

Mollie Ford, who lives on her own, provides foster care for two boys during 2010/11. The 12-year-old is only with her for 16 weeks but the 9-year-old boy stays with her for the whole year. Her qualifying amount for 2010/11 is £24,400 calculated as follows:

	£
Fixed amount	10,000
9-year-old (52 weeks x £200)	10,400
12-year-old (16 weeks x £250)	4,000
	———
2010/11 qualifying amount	£24,400

Where your receipts (fees, salaries, reward payments, allowances, etc) exceed the annual qualifying amount you can choose between paying tax on:

- your actual profits from foster caring worked out on the principles which apply for any other business; or

- profits worked out on a simplified method which is the difference between your total receipts for the year less the annual qualifying amount.

Whichever way you choose to be taxed you must at least keep records of your receipts and the ages and number of weeks that you care for each child placed with you. For this purpose a week runs from Monday to the following Sunday. Part of a week counts as a full week.

Furnished holiday accommodation

The letting of furnished holiday accommodation in both the UK and anywhere else in the European Economic Area may be treated as a trade so long as the property is:

- let commercially and furnished;

- available for letting commercially to the public as holiday accommodation for at least 140 days in a 12-month period;

- actually let for at least 70 such days; and

- not normally occupied by the same person for more than 31 consecutive days at any time during the period of 7 months within the 12-month period.

As the letting of furnished holiday accommodation is treated as a trading activity:

- you can claim capital allowances on expenditure for furniture and equipment in the holiday home; and

- you can claim relief for losses against your other income.

Other special situations

In the space available I have only been able to paint a general picture of the way in which the profits of most businesses are taxed. If you are a farmer, a writer, a Lloyds underwriter or a subcontractor in the construction industry you should know that there are special rules for working out the taxable profits from these and some other trades, professions or vocations. In such situations it is advisable to seek professional assistance.

8 NATIONAL INSURANCE AND STATE BENEFITS

Employed or self-employed, you must pay National Insurance contributions as well as Income Tax on your earnings or business profits. By paying sufficient National Insurance contributions you become eligible to claim those social security benefits which are based on your contribution history. Many benefits, mainly those payable to the disabled, do not depend upon the payment of contributions.

National Insurance numbers

You need to have a National Insurance number (NINO) so that all the contributions you make can be properly recorded. All children are usually notified of their NINO shortly before their 16th birthday and reaching school leaving age. Otherwise you can apply at any time over age 16 providing you can satisfy the requirements of residence or presence in Great Britain.

Your NINO is made up of two letters, six numbers and followed by a further letter – A, B, C or D. You will receive a plastic card (an RD3), similar to a credit card, which will be sent to your home address.

National Insurance contributions

There are four classes of contribution payable as follows:

- Class 1 by employees;
- Class 2 by the self-employed;
- Class 3 which is voluntary; and
- Class 4 by the self-employed, based on profits of your business.

You do not have to go on paying contributions once you attain State Pension age, even if you carry on working either in employment or in your own business. For a man this is currently age 65. For women born between 6 April 1950 and 5 April 1955 there is a gradual increase in State Pension age from ages 60 to 65.

(a) Class 1

The earnings of employees on which contributions are calculated include:

- a salary or wage – before deduction for pension contributions;
- overtime, bonuses and commission;
- holiday pay; and
- statutory sick, maternity and paternity pay.

Nevertheless, no contributions are payable by employees on:

- Business expenses;
- Tips and gratuities; or
- Redundancy payments.

The contributions you pay are usually a percentage of your weekly or monthly salary or wage, subject to lower- and upper-earnings limits which change from year to year. If

- you change jobs and have a break between them; or
- there is a period when you are unemployed,

the rate and amount of contribution you pay when you return to work is unaffected.

If you have more than one employment you must pay contributions on your earnings from all your jobs. However, there is an overall annual maximum limit of contributions payable by employees. You can apply for a refund in any year where the total contributions you have paid exceed this annual limit. Alternatively, by completing form CF379, you can apply for deferment where you reckon that the contributions you will pay on earnings from two or more employments will exceed the maximum annual limit. The National Insurance Contributions Office of HMRC will then instruct one or other of your employers not to withhold contributions from your earnings. After the end of the tax year your overall contribution history is reviewed. If you have not paid enough contributions the National Insurance Contributions Office will send you a calculation and a demand for the balance due.

(b) Class 2

This is a weekly flat rate payable by the self-employed. You can pay either by direct debit every four weeks or on demand every 13 weeks. If your business profits are less than a specified limit each year you are exempted from paying contributions. But you should apply in advance for what is known as small-earnings exception.

(c) Class 3

The payment of these flat-rate contributions is voluntary. They may be paid by a man under age 65 or a woman under 60 in order to preserve entitlement to some benefits and towards their contribution history for a state pension.

(d) Class 4

These are payable by the self-employed based on a percentage of taxable business profits, after capital allowances, but before relief for pension contributions. They are paid each year through the tax system along with the Income Tax due on business profits.

The profits of Dennis Cole's business, as adjusted for tax purposes, are £50,100 for 2010/11. For the same year his claim to capital allowances amounts to £16,250, giving a net chargeable amount of £33,850 for 2010/11. He pays Class 4 contributions of £2,250.80 as follows:

	£
On the first £5,715	Nil
On the next £28,135 @ 8%	2,250.80

	£2,250.80
	=========

Rates and leaflets

The rates of National Insurance contributions for 2010/11 are listed in Appendix 4 at the end of the book.

From 6th April 2011:

- the 11% rate of Employees contribution increases to 12%;

- the 1% rate paid by Employees on earnings in excess of the upper earnings limit goes up to 2%;

- the 8% levy on the profits of the self-employed between the lower and upper profits limits increases to 9%;

- above the upper profits limit the rate moves up from 1% to 2%.

Your local HMRC (National Insurance Contributions) office should be able to supply you with any leaflets or forms you need. A list of those with the widest application is in Appendix 5.

Social Security benefits

Responsibility for administering all aspects of the Social Security system lies with the Department for Work and Pensions (DWP). There are local DWP offices all across the country. The framework of the social security system is now so substantial, and the range of benefits so wide and varied, consequently it is only possible for me to give a brief summary of the main state benefits which fall into these categories:

- working-age benefits (for those under age 60), administered by Jobcentre Plus;

- pension-age benefits (for those over age 60), administered by the Pension, Disability and Carers Service;

- tax credits (see Chapter 3) for families with children and people in work, administered by HM Revenue & Customs; and

- disability and carer benefits, administered by the Pension, Disability and Carers Service.

Many benefits are only payable to individuals with an established National Insurance contribution history. The type of benefit you can claim depends on the class of contributions paid as follows:

Type of Benefit	Class 1 (Employed)	Class 2 (Self-Employed)	Class 3 (Voluntary)
Retirement Pension			
— basic	Yes	Yes	Yes
— additional	Yes	No	No
— widow's	Yes	Yes	Yes
Bereavement allowance	Yes	Yes	Yes
Bereavement payment	Yes	Yes	Yes
Widowed mother's allowance	Yes	Yes	Yes
Widowed parent's allowance	Yes	Yes	Yes
Widow's Payment	Yes	Yes	Yes
Incapacity benefit	Yes	Yes	No
Jobseeker's allowance	Yes	No	No
Employment and Support Allowance	Yes	Yes	No
Statutory Sick, Maternity and Paternity Pay	Yes	No	No

Other benefits do not depend upon the payment of contributions.

(a) Statutory sick pay

To be able to claim statutory sick pay you must be paying sufficient Class 1 contributions. Other main points are:

- it is a flat-rate cash payment made to employees by their employer;

- to claim you must be both incapable of work and not actually do any work at all on the day in question;

- it is not payable for the first three agreed qualifying days in any period when you are too unwell to work; and

- in any period of sickness you have a maximum entitlement to 28 weeks of statutory sick pay.

(b) Statutory maternity pay

Eligibility for statutory maternity pay is again dependent on the payment of Class 1 contributions. A woman:

- qualifies for statutory maternity pay if she has been working continuously for the same employer for 26 weeks up to, and including, the 15th week before her baby is due;

- must provide evidence of being pregnant and give her employer sufficient notice of leaving work; and

- will receive benefit for 39 weeks beginning not earlier than the 11th week before the baby is due, although she can actually select the time over which she will be absent from work.

(c) Statutory paternity pay

The basic features of statutory paternity pay are:

- fathers are allowed up to two weeks away from work during the first eight weeks of their child's life;

- it is also a flat-rate cash payment; and

- the qualifying requirements are the same as those for statutory maternity pay.

(d) Jobseekers allowance

The key points of the jobseekers allowance, which is taxable, are:

- it is payable to unemployed individuals between the ages of 18 and state pension age who are available for work and are actively seeking employment;

- a claimant must sign a jobseekers agreement which sets out the steps he or she intends to take towards getting full-time employment;

- entitlement is based on either a satisfactory contribution record or a means-tested low income;

- it is a weekly benefit with supplements for age and other personal circumstances; and

- an individual is disqualified from receiving benefit if he or she fails to honour the obligations of the jobseekers agreement, or refuses to follow either recommendations or directions of the employment adviser.

(e) Employment and Support Allowance

This allowance replaced Incapacity Benefit for new claimants from 27 October 2008. Anyone receiving Incapacity Benefit at that date will continue to receive it so long as they remain eligible.

You may be able to claim Employment and Support Allowance if any of the following apply:

- you are no longer receiving Statutory Sick Pay or you cannot get it;
- you are self-employed or unemployed;
- you have been receiving Statutory Maternity Pay and have not gone back to work because of illness or a disability;
- you are under State Pension age.

You must also either:

- have had an illness or disability which stops you from working for at least four days in a row (weekends and Public Holidays also count);
- you are unable to work for two or more days out of seven consecutive days;
- you are getting special medical treatment.

If you are between 16 and 20 years old (or under 25 if you were in educational training for at least three months immediately before you turned 20), you must:

- have been unable to work because of an illness or disability lasting at least 28 weeks;
- have not been able to work before you turned 20 (or 25 if you were in education or training for at least three months immediately before turning 20).

There are two types of Employment and Support allowance:

- contribution-based;
- income-related.

To be able to claim the contribution-based type you must have paid enough National Insurance contributions.

You may be able to claim income-related Employment and Support Allowance;

- if you do not have enough money coming in; or
- you have not paid enough National Insurance contributions and you satisfy the entitlement conditions.

(f) Income support

Income support is a non-contributory weekly benefit paid to individuals who do not have sufficient money to live on. The circumstances of each individual are looked at and the amounts required to meet their weekly needs are assessed. These are food, fuel, water rates, ordinary clothing and housing costs.

(g) Child benefit

Child benefit is payable:

- to individuals bringing up children;
- for all children under 16 years old; and
- for children over age 16, but under 19, providing they are still in full-time education which includes courses at school or college up to 'A' level.

It is not means-tested and for couples who are married it is the mother who should make the claim.

(h) Benefits for the disabled

These include the disability living and attendance allowances. Disability living allowance:

- is a weekly tax-free cash allowance;
- is not income related;
- is a single benefit comprising two components – mobility and care; and
- can be paid for an indefinite period, but the first claim must be made before an individual's 65th birthday.

Attendance allowance is paid to people over 65 who are seriously disabled, mentally or physically, and who need a lot of care and attention both throughout the day and at night.

Capital Limits

You will not be entitled to:

- Income Support; or
- Housing or Council Tax Benefits; or
- Income-related Jobseekers and Employment and Support allowances

if your capital is over £16,000. The amount of the above benefits you will receive is tapered where your capital is between £6,000 and £16,000. Capital includes:

- cash;
- funds held in a bank or building society account; and
- shares or investment trusts at market value or surrender rate less 10%.

Benefits and Rates

Listed in Appendix 6 at the end of the book are all the Social Security benefits, distinguishing between those which are taxable and non-taxable.

Following on is Appendix 7 which gives the rates of the main taxable Social Security benefits for 2010/11.

State Pension Credit

An individual is entitled to the State Pension Credit if he or she:

- lives in Great Britain;
- satisfies at least one of two requirements of the guarantee and savings credits respectively; and
- has reached the qualifying age.

The guarantee credit 'tops up' the income of a single claimant to £132.60 per week for 2010/11. For couples, including civil partners, the weekly income limit increases to £202.40. A claimant's income includes:

- a state and any other pension;

- earnings;

- Social Security benefits; and

- notional investment income of £1 a week for every £500 of savings or capital in excess of £10,000 (excluding your home and possessions).

The purpose of the savings credit, the rules for which are far from simple, is to reduce Pension Credit by 40% of the amount by which a pensioner's income exceeds the appropriate minimum guarantee.

The guarantee credit is available to:

- both men and women who have reached the State Pension age for women;

- a member of a couple where the other partner has attained the State Pension age for women.

The qualifying age for both men and women increases to age 65 for the savings credit element.

9   STATE AND PRIVATE PENSIONS

I don't doubt that when you give up work and retire you will want to be able to maintain your lifestyle and living standards. You may have built up savings while you were working but your income in retirement is most likely to come from:

- the State Pension; and

- an employer or personal pension scheme.

So that you can give yourself the best possible opportunity to build up a good pension you should start contributing to a plan as soon as you can reasonably afford to do so.

State Pension

There are three parts to the state retirement pension:

- the basic retirement (or old person's) pension;

- a state-earnings-related pension (SERPS/S2P); and

- a graduated pension.

(a) Basic state pension

You are entitled to a basic pension if you:

- have reached state pension age;

- satisfy the contribution requirements; and

- make a claim for the pension.

State pension age for men is age 65. For women, there is a progressive increase from age 60 to 65 depending on their date of birth between 6 April 1950 and 5 April 1955.

To receive a full basic state pension you need 30 qualifying years. Otherwise you will receive a basic pension equivalent to 1/30th of the weekly rate for each of your qualifying years.

A qualifying year is a tax year in which you have earned, or been credited with, earnings equivalent to at least 52 × the lower weekly earnings limit for National Insurance purposes.

In any year you receive certain Social Security Benefits, you will be credited with earnings up to the amount to make that year a qualifying year.

(b) SERPS/S2P

As the name implies any entitlement to the state second pension depends on your earnings while you are working and the payment of Class 1 contributions.

The additional state pension, when it was first introduced in 1978, was known as SERPS. It was reformed in 2002 as S2P to provide a more generous additional state pension for individuals on low or moderate incomes.

(c) A graduated pension

You will have earned extra state pension if you paid graduated National Insurance contributions when the scheme was in operation between April 1961 and April 1975.

(d) Additional pension benefits

A man may receive extra pension for:

- a wife;
- dependent children; or
- a woman looking after his children.

A married woman receives a retirement pension either:

- by reference to her own contributions record; or
- based on her husband's contribution if she is over age 60 and retired, providing her husband is receiving the basic retirement pension; or
- as a wife dependent on her husband. He is then entitled to an increase in his pension.

The amount of retirement pension payable to a widow will depend upon whether she was widowed before or after her normal retirement age.

Lump sums

You can defer taking your State Pension and either:

• receive an increased pension when you actually take it; or

• be paid a lump sum.

If you opt for a simple addition to your future State Pension the higher weekly payment is the amount which is taxable when you start to receive it.

Under the lump sum alternative:

• The rate of pension is that fixed at the time you apply for deferral.

• The single payment will comprise both pension arrears, including increments, and interest thereon.

• The total amount is liable to income tax.

• It is not added to income for any tax purposes.

• The tax you pay on the lump sum is worked out by applying your marginal rate of tax.

• The Pension Service will deduct tax at source based on your declaration indicating your likely band of taxable income.

• You can elect for it to be paid and, therefore, taxed in the following tax year.

• You can do this at any time from the date you choose to receive the lump sum up to one month later.

• No further interest is added to the lump sum.

• The minimum deferral period is one of 12 consecutive months. There is no maximum length of time for which drawing your State Pension can be deferred.

• In most cases the Executors of a deceased persons Estate will be able to claim any undrawn lump sum benefit that had accrued up to the date of death.

Archie Barber is now in his late 60s. He was entitled to draw his State Pension in June 2009 but decided against doing so at the time. He chose to take his lump sum, amounting to £4,400, one year later in June 2010. In 2010/11 his total pension income amounted to £12,000 and he received gross interest on his building society account of £800, He pays tax of £880 on his lump sum as follows:

	£
Pensions	12,000
Building Society interest	800
	12,800
Less: Personal age allowance	9,490
Taxable income	£3,310
2010/11 tax due: £3,310 x 20%	£662
Tax payable on lump sum State Pension: £4,400 x 20% (as a 20% tax payer)	£880

State Pension Forecast

You can get a state pension forecast if you are more than four months away from state pension age when your application is processed. Your forecast will advise you in today's money of the amounts of the three parts to the state retirement pension already earned. It will also tell you:

- what further state pension you might earn before you retire; and

- if there is anything you can do to improve your basic state pension.

The application form, BR19, is available from the Pension Service by telephoning 0845 3000 168. Alternatively, the forecast can be obtained online.

Private Pensions

There are a number of attractions in saving for your retirement through a private pension plan. If you are self-employed you will need to make your own arrangements. For those of you working in employment it is more than likely that your employer is running a scheme for the employees of the business which you can join.

The main features of pension provision are:

- You receive full tax relief on your premiums.

- Your contributions are invested in a tax-free fund.

- You can take your benefits at any time between the ages of 55 and 75.

- You do not have to retire to access your benefits.

- 25% of the value of your fund can be paid to you as a tax-free lump sum.

(a) Annual contributions

You can get tax relief on pension contributions up to 100% of your annual earnings, subject to a maximum annual allowance which is £255,000 for 2010/11. Non-earners and non-taxpayers can put up to £3,600 before tax each year into pension savings.

As the tax relief on pension contributions for individuals with incomes over £150,000 is restricted from 6 April 2011 measures were introduced to prevent individuals obtaining higher rate tax relief on the payment of substantial additional pension premiums in the intervening period from 22 April 2009 to 5 April 2011.

Under these rules:

- an individual with an income of more than £150,000;

- still receives full tax relief on premiums above £20,000;

- as long as the amount or payment pattern of the contributions doesn't change significantly from that in place on Budget Day 2009.

But if the same individual:

- has an income of at least £150,000 in the current or two previous tax years;

- makes annual pension contributions of more than £20,000; and

- alters their pattern of payment.

Premiums paid of more than £20,000 will only qualify for tax relief at the basic rate.

(b) Lifetime allowance

There is a single lifetime allowance on the amount of your pension savings that can benefit from tax relief. This limit was £1.8 million from April 2010 but it goes up each year. If the value of your pension fund is more than the lifetime allowance when you come to draw your pension you will be subject to tax on the excess.

(c) Transitional provisions

There are transitional arrangements to protect pension rights built up before 6 April 2006, including two options for transitional protection from the lifetime allowance tax charge.

(d) Death benefits

These can be in the form of:

- a lump sum;

- a pension for one or more dependents; or

- a combination of lump sum and pension.

10 SAVINGS AND INVESTMENT INCOME

There are likely to be occasions during your lifetime when you will either be:

- making regular savings out of income;

- investing a lump sum from a pension scheme on retirement; or

- in receipt of a much more substantial sum such as an inheritance or, perhaps, winnings on the National Lottery.

Examples of savings and investment income are:

- bank or building society interest;

- share and unit trust dividends;

- rents;

- interest on government stocks; and

- income from a trust fund.

Tax free income

The most widely known investments where the return is tax free are some of those available from National Savings and Investments. They are:

- Fixed-Interest and Index-Linked Savings Certificates;

- Children's Bonus Bonds; and

- Premium Bond Prizes.

Also tax free are:

- interest on your cash ISAs;

- dividends from your ISA investments; and

- dividends paid on your shares in Venture Capital Trusts.

Tax free income does not need to be reported on your annual Income Tax Return.

Interest and dividends

You will receive dividends on your shares or interest on your bank/building society accounts or British Government stocks either:

- with a 10% tax credit which cannot be reclaimed;

- less Income Tax at 20%; or

- with no deduction for tax.

*Interest is always paid with no deduction for tax on the following holdings:

Non-repayable 10% tax credit	Tax deducted at 20%	No tax deducted
Dividends on shares	Bank and building society interest	National Savings: • Easy Access Savings Account • Investment Account • Income Bonds
Income distributions on unit trust holdings	National Savings Guaranteed Growth and Income Bonds	*Interest on British Government Stocks
	*Interest on British Government Stocks with some exceptions	Tax Deposit Certificates
	Income element of purchased life annuities	Single Deposits over £50,000 for a fixed period of less than five years
		Deposits with non-UK branches of banks and building societies

- 3.5% War Loan.
- Government Stocks held on the National Savings and Investments Register.

You can, if you want, choose to receive the interest on all other holdings of British Government stocks with no tax deducted. However, if the interest is being paid to you after deduction of tax and you would prefer to receive it with no tax deducted you will have to write to Computershare to request this change.

In working out how much tax you have to pay each year, dividend and interest income is always regarded as the top part of your income. If you have both dividend and interest (savings) income your dividends will be treated as the highest part. As a result:

- Non-taxpayers can only claim for a repayment of Income Tax on savings income where tax at 20% has been deducted before payment. The 10% tax credit on their dividend income is non-repayable.

Tanya Bridge, who is married to Derek, receives total investment income of £3,900 during 2010/11. £3,000 is the interest on her various building society accounts – £3,750 gross with tax of £750 (20%) taken off at source – and dividends of £900 (£1,000 gross less a 10% tax credit of £100).

Tanya's total income is less than her personal allowance of £6,475 but she can only claim back from HMRC the tax of £750 suffered on her interest income.

- Individuals able to benefit from the 10% starting rate of savings income are able to reclaim some of the tax at 20% deducted at source on this income.

Tanya's sister, Henrietta, earns £4,100 from part-time employment during 2010/11. All her savings are invested in cash deposits where she receives the interest with tax deducted and during the year it comes to £2,400. Her tax repayment for the year is £537.50 as follows:

	Gross income £	Tax suffered £
Employment earnings	4,100	–
Interest income	3,000	600.00
	7,100	600.00
Less: Personal allowance	6,475	
Taxable income	£625	
Tax thereon: £625 at 10%		62.50
Repayment for 2010/11		£537.50

- Taxpayers liable at the basic rate of 20%, but neither the higher or additional rates, do not pay any further tax on their dividend and interest income.

Tanya's aunt, Davina, receives building society interest, including tax deducted at source, of £1,200 in 2010/11. Her earned income, after allowances and reliefs, comes to £10,000. She pays tax for the year as follows:

on her earned income of	£10,000 @ 20%
on her interest income of	£1,200 @ 20%

- Individuals whose income takes them into the higher rate of 40% must pay Income Tax of a further 20% on their non-dividend savings income above the basic-rate band. If the income beyond the basic-rate band comes from dividends the extra tax payable is at 22.5% on the total of dividends and their tax credits.

Tanya's husband, Derek, banks interest and dividend income amounting to £9,000 (gross) and £2,600 (including the 10% tax credit) respectively during 2010/11. His earnings, after allowances and reliefs, total £30,000. His tax charge is worked out as follows:

on his earned income of	£30,000 @ 20%
on his interest income of	£7,400 @ 20%
on his interest income of	£1,600 @ 40%
on his dividends	£2,600 @ 32.5%

The £7,400 slice of interest income attracts tax at the rate of 20% as it falls within the limit of income of £37,400 taxed at the basic rate.

Individuals not liable to tax can arrange to receive their interest gross. This is done by completing special forms which are available at banks, building societies, post offices and tax offices throughout the country as well as from the HMRC website.

Accrued income

Interest on fixed-rate investments is regarded as accruing from day-to-day between payment dates. On a sale the vendor is charged Income Tax on the interest that has accrued from the previous payment date to the date of sale. The purchaser is allowed to deduct this amount from the interest received on the following payment date.

These arrangements cover both fixed and variable-rate stocks and bonds, including those issued by Governments, companies and local authorities. But the arrangements will not affect you if the nominal value of your securities is under £5,000.

The interest on a holding of 8% Treasury Stock 2013 is payable on each 27 March and 27 September. The half-yearly interest on a holding of £20,000, sold for settlement on 16 July 2010, is £1,000.

$$\text{Accrued proportion} = \frac{111}{183} \times £1,000 = £606.56$$

Rents

The letting of property, including isolated or casual lettings, is treated as a business for tax purposes. This applies to any flat, house, shop or other property that you rent to tenants. Most of the rules for working out the taxable profits from a trade or profession are also relevant in working out your annual income from the letting of property. Income from all your properties in the UK is pooled together, regardless of the type of lease. Also it does not matter whether the property is let furnished or unfurnished.

However, unlike a trade or profession, losses from your property rental business can only be carried forward to be set against future profits from the same activities.

Other than expenditure of a capital nature, such as that on extensions, structural alterations or improvements, the general running costs of a property can be set against rental income. Included in allowable expenses are:

- fees incurred on letting out the property, including estate agents' costs, advertisements and the fees for drawing up an inventory;

- rent collection and management costs;
- interest relating to your property letting business. It does not matter whether the interest is payable on a loan or overdraft;
- maintenance, repairs and redecorations;
- insurance premiums on buildings and contents policies;
- rents and water rates;
- council tax paid for your tenants;
- gardening, cleaning and security services;
- all other expenses of managing the property such as stationery, postage, advertising for tenants etc; and
- your share of expenditure on the common parts of the let property.

If you improve the energy use of a residential property which you let out you can claim a deduction against your rents for expenditure of up to £1,500 spent on each dwelling house for:

- loft, wall or floor insulation;
- draught proofing; and/or
- insulating the hot water system.

These costs would normally be treated as improvements. As such they could not be offset against rental income without this special tax relief.

Karen Donnelly owns a flat which she let out to tenants during 2010/11. The net rental income for the year amounts to £14,740 as follows:

	£	£
Rent receivable from the flat		21,000
Less: *Expenses*		
Agents fees for letting	2,467	
Management fees	740	
Ground rent	200	
Service charges	1,103	
Council tax for tenants	960	
Water rates	220	
Lounge redecoration	490	
Boiler repair	80	
	—–––––	6,260
2010/11 net rental income		£14,740

Where you are renting out:

- Unfurnished property, you can claim capital allowances on the cost of fixtures, fittings and equipment spent on the let property.

- Furnished property, you are allowed an additional deduction to cover the cost of wear and tear to furnishings and fittings which can be what you actually spend on renewing them. Alternatively you can claim a fixed allowance equivalent to 10% of the rent you receive less amounts paid out on Council Tax and water rates.

If Karen's flat in the preceding illustration had been let furnished this allowance would amount to £1,982 as follows:

	£
Rent receivable	21,000
Less: Council Tax and water rates	1,180
	£19,820
Wear and tear allowance: 10%	£1,982

The rules dealing with the taxation of premiums on leases are more complicated and outside the scope of this book.

Rent-a-Room

Income from the furnished letting of spare rooms in your home as residential accommodation is tax free providing the gross rents do not exceed £4,250 per annum. The space you let out must be in your only or main home which can be a house, flat, caravan or even a houseboat.

You can elect to opt out of this special form of relief. It will pay you to make the opt-out election if, for example, there is a loss on the letting which can be set against your other rental profits under the normal rules dealing with income from lettings.

Where your annual gross rents are more than £4,250 you must elect if you want to pay tax on the excess gross rents, without any relief for expenses. If you do not do so then you will have to work out your taxable income using the rules for lettings income.

Theresa Stevens is a basic-rate taxpayer who lets out a room in her bungalow to a lodger paying £110 per week, £5,720 for 2010/11. The expenses that could be set against the lodger's rents total £1,600 for the year.

Theresa elects for Rent-a-Room relief and her Income Tax liability is £294.00 (£5,720 - £4,250) x 20%. Under the normal rules her tax liability would come to £824.00 (£5,720 – £1,600) x 20%.

The tax-free limit of £4,250 is halved where an individual and some other person are each entitled to income under the scheme. Each lessor's exempt amount is then £2,125.

Non-qualifying life policies

At the outset, a lump sum premium is paid into a Bond which is, for example, either investment based or intended to produce a guaranteed income. An investor can usually:

- take regular amounts out;

- make ad hoc partial withdrawals; or

- leave the Bond untouched until encashment or death when it will form part of the investor's estate.

There is no tax relief on the single premium. Neither Capital Gains Tax nor Income Tax at the savings rate is payable on any profit. But investors whose income takes them into either the higher or additional rates of 40% or 50% will pay tax at the difference between their top rate and the basic rate of Income Tax on chargeable events. These arise on:

- surrender or maturity of the policy;

- death of the life assured; or

- withdrawals in excess of a cumulative allowance built up at the time.

At the end of each policy year an allowance of 5% of the original investment is given. This can be carried forward from year to year. Over a period of 20 years, allowances of up to 100% of the initial investment will be given. A taxable gain only arises if the amount of the withdrawal is more than the cumulative allowance at the time. Then it is the excess which is taxed.

Edward Clark invests £15,000 in an Investment Bond. Withdrawals of £600, £900 and £3,250 are made during the second, third and fifth policy years. The annual allowance is £750 being 5%, of the original investment. A taxable gain of £1,000 arises in year five as follows:

Number of Policy Years	Cumulative Allowance	Amount Withdrawn	Cumulative Withdrawals	Taxable Amount
	£	£	£	£
1	750	—	—	—
2	1,500	600	600	—
3	2,250	900	1,500	—
4	3,000	—	1,500	—
5	3,750	3,250	4,750	1,000

When the final chargeable event on a Bond occurs, the taxable gain is calculated by taking into account all previous withdrawals and taxable gains.

After seven years, Edward encashes the Investment Bond in the illustration above for £21,050. The taxable gain amounts to £9,800 as follows:

	£	£
Policy proceeds		21,050
Add: Withdrawals in years 2, 3 and 5		4,750
		25,800
Less: Original investment	15,000	
Amount already taxed	1,000	
		16,000
Taxable gain on encashment		£9,800

The method of calculating the Income Tax due on the taxable gain involves a number of stages, including 'top slicing' relief.

Edward is a single man. During 2010/11 his other income, all earnings, amounted to £43,475. He pays tax of £1,399.44 on the gain of £9,800 on the final encashment of his Bond worked out as follows:

Gain on encashment of Bond	£9,800
Number of years held	7
Taxable slice of gain	£1,400
Taxable income – excluding slice of gain	
Earnings	43,475
Less: Personal allowance	6,475
	£37,000
Tax applicable to slice of gain	
On first £400 (£37,400 – £37,000) @ 0%	—
On next £1,000 (excess over £37,400) @ 20% (40% – 20%)	£200.00
Average rate on slice	14.28%
The tax payable on the gain = £9,800 @ 14.28% =	£1,399.44

Individual Savings Accounts

An Individual Savings Account (ISA) can include up to two components:

- cash (including National Savings); and
- stocks and shares.

You can subscribe to an ISA if you are:

- both resident and ordinarily resident in the UK for tax purposes; and
- aged 18 or over, although 16- and 17-year-olds can invest in just the cash component.

The annual subscription limit for all qualifying individuals is:

- £10,200 of which no more than £5,100 can go into cash; and

- is increased each year in line with the Retail Prices Index rounded to a convenient multiple of £120 to allow for the easy calculation of monthly contributions.

Other features of an ISA are:

- The account is completely free of tax.

- There is no statutory lock-in period or minimum subscription. You can make withdrawals whenever you like.

- There is no lifetime investment limit.

- Savers can transfer money saved in cash ISAs into stocks and shares ISAs.

The list of investments which qualify for the stocks and shares component include:

- shares listed on a recognized Stock Exchange;

- Unit Trusts;

- Investment Trusts;

- open-ended investment companies; and

- Government stocks with at least five years to go to maturity.

Each year savers have two choices when it comes to appointing their plan managers. The first option allows them to go to a single manager who offers an account that can accept the overall subscription. This means that:

- the account includes the stocks and shares component, but does not need to offer cash;

- savers can subscribe up to £10,200 for stocks and shares; and

- if, in addition, the plan manager offers the cash component, savers can deposit up to £5,100 in cash, and the un-invested balance can go into stocks and shares.

Under the second option savers can go to separate managers – one for each component – and:

- up to £5,100 can be saved in cash;

- the remainder of the annual allowance can be invested in stocks and shares.

Enterprise Investment Scheme

The aims of the Scheme are twofold:

- To provide a targeted incentive for equity investment in unquoted trading companies which help overcome the problems faced by such companies in raising modest amounts of equity finance.

- To encourage outside investors previously unconnected with the company, who introduce finance and expertise, by allowing them actively to participate in the management of the company as paid directors without losing entitlement to relief.

The main features of the Scheme are:

- Income Tax relief at 20% on qualifying investments up to £500,000 in a tax year;

- subject to the annual £500,000 subscription limit the Income Tax relief can be carried back to the previous year;

- all shares in a qualifying company must be held for at least three years; otherwise the Income Tax relief will be clawed back; and

- losses made on the disposal of qualifying shares are eligible for relief from either Income Tax or Capital Gains Tax.

Venture Capital Trusts

Venture Capital Trusts (VCTs) are a type of Investment Trust with tax advantages designed to encourage investment in the under-nourished small-business sector. Individuals investing in VCTs are eligible for the following Income Tax incentives:

- relief at 30% on subscriptions for new ordinary shares up to £200,000 in any tax year, providing the shares are held for at least five years; and

- tax free dividends.

The 30% income tax relief is deductible from the total income tax payable and does not depend on the investing individual's marginal tax rate.

Overseas investment income

Generally, income from investments or savings abroad is taxed in the same way as your onshore dividends or interest income. Foreign tax paid, subject to certain restrictions, can be offset against the tax payable here on the same income. If required, you must be able to show that you have actually paid, or suffered, the overseas tax.

Joint income

Income from assets such as bank/building society accounts, property or shares held in the joint names of a married couple or civil partners is treated for tax purposes as belonging to them in equal proportions. If the actual proportions of ownership between the couple are unequal they can make an election for the income on any jointly owned assets to be taxed in accordance with their respective entitlements to the income. There is a special form to complete. The declaration applies from the date it is made.

But dividends from jointly owned shares in a small family company are taxed on husband and wife according to their actual ownership, rather than in equal shares.

In view of:

- the restriction to the personal allowance for individuals with incomes of more than £100,000; and

- the 50% rate of Income Tax on incomes in excess of £150,000;

income splitting is likely to be of relevance to some taxpayers as a means of reducing their overall tax burden.

11   THE FAMILY UNIT

Gone are the days when it was commonplace for couples to marry. Many now prefer to live together as partners. Opposite-sex couples may even have children without marrying or marry later on in life.

Living together

There are no special tax breaks for couples living with one another as partners. They are each taxed as single people. Furthermore, it is mandatory that income from jointly owned assets must be split between them in accordance with the ratio of their respective interests in such assets. Assets cannot be transferred between them without avoiding a possible liability to Capital Gains Tax at the time of transfer.

Marriage

Husband and wife:

- are taxed separately on their income and capital gains;
- are each entitled to personal allowances which can be set against their own income, whether from earnings or investments;
- can each have taxable income, after allowances and reliefs of £37,400 for 2010/11 before either of them is liable to tax at the higher rate of 40%. They may, of course, need to rearrange their affairs to take maximum advantage of potential tax savings. In contrast to the position of unmarried couples this is easily done;
- must complete their own Tax Returns every year; and
- are each responsible for settling their respective tax liabilities.

These rules also apply to same-sex couples who have legalized their relationship by forming a Civil Partnership.

Children

A child is:

- treated as an individual for tax purposes like anyone else;
- entitled to the personal allowance, so no tax is probably payable on any earnings from, for example, a daily paper round;
- also a taxable person for the purposes of Capital Gains Tax (Chapter 13) and Inheritance Tax (Chapter 17).

But, the income from a gift by a parent in favour of an unmarried minor child is regarded as the parents' income for tax purposes – subject to an annual £100 limit for small amounts of income. Grandparents or other relatives can, however, give savings to their grandchildren or nieces, nephews, etc, without the same restrictions applying to the taxation of income on any such gifts.

Savers such as children, who are not taxpayers, can elect to receive gross interest on their bank or building society accounts. As an alternative to this type of investment for your child's savings, why not take a look at the Children's Bonus Bonds issued by National Savings and Investments which are particularly suitable for investing gifts from parents. The return on these Bonds is exempt from both Income Tax and Capital Gains Tax.

There is no general tax allowance for children. However:

- you should be able to claim Child Benefit and may be due Child Tax Credit (see Chapter 3); or
- depending on your personal circumstances you may be entitled to one or more of the numerous other Social Security benefits associated with children.

It is down to parents or guardians to complete and sign Tax Returns or Repayment Claims for their children up to age 18.

The Child Trust Fund

The Child Trust Fund (CTF) is a savings and investment plan for children born before 1 January 2011.

The main features of continuing accounts existing then are:

* up to £1,200 each year can be added to the fund by family and friends;
* all income and capital growth within a CTF is tax free; and
* it can be accessed at age 18.

There are a wide range of organizations offering CTF accounts linked to either cash deposits, unit trusts or even equities.

Separation and divorce

Not only does the breakdown of a marriage cause much personal suffering but it invariably has consequences for tax purposes.

A married couple are no longer considered to be living together when:

* they are separated by a Deed or Court Order; or
* they are living apart in such a way that permanent separation is inevitable.

If a married couple are entitled to the married couple's allowance, the full allowance can be claimed by the husband for the tax year in which the marriage fails, but if he remarries in the same year he cannot also claim that part of the allowance due for the period following the wedding.

Maintenance payments are tax free in the hands of the recipient, but only limited tax relief is available to the payer of maintenance under a Court Order, Child Support Agency assessment or written agreement as follows:

* either the payer or recipient must be born before 6 April 1935;
* the payment must be to the divorced or separated spouse;
* the maximum amount of tax relief to which the payer is entitled is 10% of the lesser of £2,670 or the actual maintenance paid each year; and
* no tax relief can be claimed on maintenance paid to, or for the benefit of, children of the marriage.

The tax implications for civil partners who separate are no different to those for a married couple. Similarly the dissolution of a Civil Partnership has the same consequences as a divorce of an opposite-sex couple.

Old age

When it comes to tax, getting older does not mean an easier life. Pensioners have to deal with the tax system in the same way as everyone else. Nevertheless, there are some factors which are only relevant to:

- the finances of elderly persons; and
- working out how much tax they must pay each year.

First and foremost come the age allowances. In Chapter 2, I explained how a pensioner calculates the amount of these allowances to which he or she is entitled.

Men qualify to receive the State Pension when they reach age 65; for women this date depends on when they were born between 6 April 1950 and 5 April 1955. The State Pension includes:

- the basic retirement (or old person's) pension;
- a state earnings-related pension (SERPS/S2P);
- a graduated pension; and
- the age addition if you are over 80.

On reaching retirement age a pensioner has three options:

- retire and claim the state pension;
- carry on working and claim the state pension; or
- put off taking the state pension.

If you choose to defer taking your state pension you can claim:

- additional state pension when you eventually retire; or
- a lump sum – equal to the state pension to which you would have been entitled during the period of deferment, plus compound interest.

All pensions, including a State Pension, are taxable. There is, however, no mechanism to deduct any Income Tax at source from payment of the State Pension. Therefore, in addition to including a pensioner's personal allowance in the coding notice of an occupational or personal pension taxed under PAYE, it also incorporates a deduction from allowances equivalent to the annual amount of the State Pension. In this way:

- the tax due on the State Pension is collected; and
- the need to make a direct tax payment is avoided.

The significance of the following letters at the end of a Code Number is as follows:

- P – indicates the full personal allowance is due for those aged 65–74.
- Y – means you are due the full personal allowance for age 75 and over.
- T – applies in most other circumstances.

If a pensioner's State Pension and other deductions exceeds his or her personal allowance, HMRC issue a 'K' Coding. The amount of the negative allowance is then added to the pension on which tax is paid.

Taxpayers approaching State Pension age should make sure that their Notice of Coding is changed to include an estimate of the amount of their State Pension for the year. Usually HMRC sends such taxpayers a Form P161 asking for details about pension entitlement. This information is then used to amend tax codes as appropriate.

Nowadays many people carry on working after they retire from their main job or self-employment. They may decide to make use of all the knowledge and experience built up during their working lives by setting up in business as a consultant, or take a part-time position in, for example, a retail outlet.

Owen Wilcox is single and 68. During 2010/11 he received a State Pension of £95.25 per week and an annual pension from his previous employer of £8,000. To keep himself occupied he worked part-time at his local DIY Store, earning a weekly wage of £105 for 46 weeks of the year. Owen paid Income Tax for 2010/11 of £1,658.60 as follows:

	Income £	Tax £
State Pension	4,953	
Occupational Pension	8,000	692.60
Wages	4,830	966.00
	17,783	£1,658.60
Less: Personal Allowance	9,490	
Taxable Income	£8,293	
Income Tax payable		
£8,293 @ 20%		£1,658.60

The tax code used for working out the Income Tax to be deducted from Owen's occupational pension is 453P. This is based on the difference between Owen's personal age allowance of £9,490 and his State Pension of £4,953. Tax at the basic rate of 20%, under a BR Code, would have been deducted from Owen's wage from the DIY store.

To gain maximum advantage from the personal age and married couple's allowance, elderly married couples with modest incomes may need to transfer capital between themselves.

Bert and Mavis Wilkins, a married couple, both in their late 70s, whose joint income for 2010/11 amounted to £50,000, paid Income Tax of £6,437 on this sum. This mainly related to Bert's income as follows:

	Bert	Mavis
	£	£
State Pensions	5,077	2,802
Occupational Pensions	16,923	6,108
Building Society Interest		
Gross equivalent	11,000	1,890
Interest on British Government Stocks	5,000	1,200
	38,000	12,000
Less: Personal Allowance	6,475	9,640
Taxable Income	£31,525	£2,360
Income Tax Payable		
£—/£730 @ 10%	—	73
£31,525/£1,630 @ 20%	6,305	326
	6,305	399
Less: Relief for married couple's		
allowance – £2,670 @ 10%	267	—
	£6,038	£399

Bert's income is above the upper limit for entitlement to either personal age or married couple's allowances.

Significant tax savings of £512.50 for 2010/11 could have been achieved by the couple if Bert had transferred capital to Mavis as follows:

	Bert	Mavis
	£	£
State Pensions	5,077	2,802
Occupational Pensions	16,923	6,108
Building Society Interest		
Gross equivalent	2,600	10,290
Interest on British Government Stocks	1,400	4,800
	26,000	24,000
Less: Personal Allowance	7,940	8,940
Taxable Income	£18,060	£15,060
Income Tax payable		
£—/£30 @ 10%	—	3.00
£18,060/£15,030 @ 20%	3,612.00	3,006.00
	3,612.00	3,009.00
Less: Relief for married couple's		
allowance – £6,965 @ 10%	696.50	—
	£2,915.50	£3,009.00

Death

Sadly, death comes to all of us and has tax consequences for married couples which are:

- the married couple's allowance is not restricted in the year of death of either spouse;

- where the husband dies first, he is due his full personal allowance in the year of death. If he cannot use up the full married couple's allowance, because he has a low income, then the balance can be transferred to his widow; or

- if the wife dies before her husband she will be due her full personal allowance in the year of death.

Civil partners are treated no differently.

12   RESIDENCE AND DOMICILE

As a general rule Income Tax is charged by the United Kingdom (UK) on:

- an individual's income arising in the UK irrespective of whether that person is resident here;

- overseas income belonging to an individual resident in the UK.

Apart from some special cases, the amount of tax you pay each year depends on:

- whether you are resident and/or ordinarily resident in the UK; and

- in some circumstances on your domicile.

Not only are the two concepts of residence and domicile of fundamental importance in working out an individual's liability to UK taxation on income, but they are equally relevant for the purposes of both Capital Gains Tax and Inheritance Tax.

Residence

The UK tax legislation does not contain any statutory definition of residence and ordinary residence. The guidance and practice adopted by HMRC in determining an individual's UK residence status can be found in the booklet HMRC6 "Residence, Domicile and the Remittance Basis". What follows is a summary of the main criteria that will determine an individual's residence status.

You must normally be physically present in the UK at some point in time in the tax year before you can be regarded as resident. Without exception you will always be UK resident if you spend 183 days or more here in a tax year. You simply count up the total number of days you are in the UK. This could be:

- just a visit of 183 days or more; or

- as a result of a number of trips here.

In working out your time in the UK you must count all the days you were here at midnight.

Even if you spend less than 183 days here you will still be treated as UK resident if:

- you come here regularly; and

- after four tax years your time spent in the UK averages 91 days or more in a tax year.

From the fifth year you are treated as UK resident.

But you could become UK resident before you have been visiting the UK for four years if:

- You know at the outset that your annual visits will average out at more than 90 days. You will be treated as resident from 6 April in a tax year when you first start coming to the UK.

- You realise after starting to visit regularly that you will be spending at least 91 days on average. You will be regarded as resident from 6 April in that tax year.

However, you cannot just rely on the four year day count in determining your UK residency status. There are other factors which HMRC will look at. These are your links with the UK as follows:

- availability of accommodation;

- business interests;

- social connections; and

- family ties.

Short-term visitors need to be careful that they do not unintentionally become UK resident because of:

- their habitual pattern of visiting the UK;

- the number of days spent in the UK each year; and

- the extent of their social, family or business connections.

Ordinary Residence

Ordinary residence is:

- different from residence; and

- indicates that your residence in the UK is typical and not casual.

You do not need to have decided to stay in the UK permanently or indefinitely to become ordinarily resident. It is sufficient if your residence here has all the following attributes:

- you have come to the UK voluntarily;

- your presence here is for a settled purpose; and

- your presence in the UK forms part of the regular and habitual mode of your life for the time being.

Having ordinary residence status is, however, only generally relevant if you have foreign income during a tax year.

Working out annual average visits

The set method for working out the average number of days spent here in the UK tax year is:

$$\frac{\text{total visits to the UK (in days)}}{\text{total period since leaving (in days)}} \times 365 \text{ days} = \text{annual average visits}$$

Douglas Arrowsmith, a retired engineer, left the UK on 5 November 2009. Between the date of his departure and 5 April 2010 he spent 33 days in the UK. In the following tax year, 2010/11, he was here for 70 days. At that stage the average number of days in the UK works out at 72.85 as follows:

$$\frac{33 + 70}{151 + 365} = \frac{103}{516} \times 365 = 72.85$$

The maximum period over which the average is taken is four years, including the year of departure. This is dropped from the calculation after the third review. At each subsequent end of tax year review the oldest year is always removed from the calculation. As a result there is always a rolling period of four tax years under review.

Working abroad

Better job prospects outside the UK might make you think about looking for work overseas. This is likely to involve living away from home for a time. Your residence status in such circumstances is as follows:

'If you leave the UK to work full time abroad under a contract of employment, you are treated as not resident and not ordinarily resident if you meet all the following conditions:

- your absence from the UK and your employment abroad both last for at least a whole tax year;

- during your absence any visits you make to the UK:

  — total less than 183 days in any tax year, and

  — average less than 91 days a tax year (the average is taken over the period of absence up to a maximum of four years; any dates spent in the UK because of exceptional circumstances beyond your control, for example the illness of yourself or a member of your immediate family, are not normally counted for this purpose).

Should you meet all of the above conditions you are treated as not resident and not ordinarily resident in the UK from the day after you leave the UK to the date before you return to the UK at the end of your employment abroad. You are treated as coming to the UK permanently on the day you return from your employment abroad and as resident and ordinarily resident from that date.'

There is no precise definition of when employment abroad is 'full-time'. Nevertheless, it will be regarded as full-time if:

- your employment involves a standard pattern of hours each week which are comparable with those that would be worked in the UK; or

- you have several part-time jobs all at the same time, perhaps with the same employer or group of companies.

If you leave the UK to work full-time in a trade, profession or vocation overseas your UK residence status will be determined in the same way as anyone taking up full-time employment providing, of course, you fulfil the necessary conditions.

You may well take your spouse with you. Even if your spouse does not work abroad he or she may, by concession, also be regarded as neither resident nor ordinarily resident for the same period.

Working abroad – expenses

Tax relief is allowed on the costs you incur on travel expenses in relation to your overseas employment. Nor will you be taxed on the following expenses borne by your employer:

- The cost of board and lodging outside the UK.

- Your travelling expenses which also extends to unlimited return visits to the UK during longer assignments abroad.

- The travelling expenses of your spouse and children to visit you overseas. Not more than two return visits by the same person are allowed each year and you must be working abroad for a continuous period of at least 60 days.

Leaving the UK permanently

Where you go abroad to live:

- permanently; or

- outside the UK for three years or more,

you will become neither UK resident nor ordinarily resident from the day following your departure providing:

- you have actually physically departed; and

- have left for the reasons given to HMRC.

You should be prepared to provide sufficient evidence, such as the acquisition of a new home overseas, of your intention to make a permanent life somewhere outside the UK.

Before you leave, ask your tax office for the special form (P85) which is relevant to individuals going abroad. The information you give on the form will enable HMRC to consider your residence position. You may also be due a tax refund because you are:

- entitled to full allowances and reliefs for the year of your departure; and/or

- claiming split-year treatment.

After you have left the country, your UK resident and ordinary resident status will be affected by a number of circumstances including:

- The reason you left in the first place (for example, to work or live abroad permanently);

- What visits you make to the UK after you have gone.

- What connections you keep here such as family, property, business and social ties.

If you normally live in the UK and just are abroad for short periods – for example, to holiday or for business reasons – you will continue to be UK resident here.

When you establish not UK ordinarily resident status you can apply to receive payment of the following UK sources of interest without deduction of tax:

- on a bank or building society account;

- certain UK Government securities.

Allowances for non-UK residents

If you are not resident here, but have taxable income in the UK, you may be able to reduce your tax bill by claiming UK tax allowances. These will generally be the same as those granted to an individual resident in the UK and can be claimed by the following individuals:

- a national of a state within the European Economic Area;

- a present or former employee of the British Crown;

- a resident of the Isle of Man or the Channel Islands;

- a widow or widower of a Crown Servant;

- a person employed by a missionary society;

- a person abroad for health reasons following UK residence.

Non-resident Commonwealth citizens may be able to claim UK tax allowances under the Double Taxation Agreement concluded between the country where they are resident and the UK.

Income from UK property

Many individuals rent out their homes while they are living or working overseas. You can apply to HMRC for a certificate authorising your tenant, or managing agent, to make payments of rent to you without withholding any UK tax. If you do not apply for a certificate or one is not issued to you, tax at the basic rate must be withheld from all remittances of rent to you by your managing agent or tenant.

Whether or not tax is deducted by your tenant or letting agent, while you are non-UK resident you are still liable to UK tax on income arising from the letting out of your property here.

However, you will not actually have to pay any UK tax if:

- your income from property after allowable expenses; and

- any other taxable income

is less than any allowances that you may be entitled to claim.

Double taxation relief

If you move to a country with which the UK has concluded a Double Taxation Agreement, you may be able to claim partial or full exemption from UK tax on certain types of income such as:

- pensions and annuities;

- royalties and dividends.

Furthermore, many Double Taxation Agreements contain clauses dealing with the special circumstances of:

- teachers and researchers;

- students and apprentices;

- entertainers and sportsmen / women.

Going abroad – Capital Gains Tax

If:

- you have been resident in the UK for at least four out of the last seven years ending with the day before you leave; and

- within five years, you return here to take up residence for tax purposes again,

the concessionary split-year tax treatment does not apply for the purposes of Capital Gains Tax. You will be classified as UK tax resident for the entire tax years of both departure and return.

It follows that:

- gains realized in the tax year of departure will be taxed in that year;

- all gains in subsequent years, including the year of return, will be subject to tax in the year when residence resumes.

However, profits made on assets bought and sold during the years of non-UK tax residence will be tax-free in the UK.

Coming to the UK permanently

Perhaps:

- you have been working overseas, your contract has finished and you have decided to return home; or

- you live abroad and have accepted a job offer in the UK.

You will be treated as UK resident and ordinarily resident from the date of your arrival if you intend:

- to come to the UK to live permanently, or

- to come and remain here for three years or more.

You should:

- let HMRC know when you arrive in the UK; and

- apply for a National Insurance number (NINO) if you do not already have one and intend to work here.

You can claim full UK personal allowances for the year of arrival. Where your job is with either a UK or an overseas employer, and the duties of that employment will be performed wholly in the UK, the full amount of your salary will be taxable here.

Before you leave the country where you have been living there may be opportunities to save on UK tax before taking up residence here. For example, it may pay you to close any bank or building society accounts before arrival as you would otherwise face the prospect of a charge to UK Income Tax on interest accrued, but not credited, while abroad.

Domicile

Domicile is a concept of general law. It is distinct from residence or nationality.

When you are born you acquire a domicile of origin from your father. Until you are 16 years old your domicile follows that of the person on whom you are legally dependant. At age 16 you have the ability to abandon your existing domicile in favour of a domicile of choice. To do so you must sever all links and leave your current country or state and settle elsewhere. You will need to provide good evidence of your intention to live there indefinitely or permanently.

A wife's domicile is not necessarily the same as her husband's domicile if they were married after the end of 1973. It is governed by the same factors as for any other individual with an independent domicile. However, a woman who married before the beginning of 1974 automatically acquired her husband's domicile on marriage. So long as the marriage lasts, her domicile only alters when there is any change in the domicile of her husband.

Taxation of non-domiciliaries

An adult non-UK domiciled taxpayer:

- who has been resident in the UK for at least seven of the previous nine tax years;
- is claiming to be taxed on remittances of income to the UK;
- will lose their entitlement to the personal allowance on income and the annual exempt limit on capital gains;

- will have to pay an annual charge of £30,000 in order to claim the remittance basis unless unremitted foreign income and gains are less then a de minimus limit of £2,000;

- claims non-UK domiciled status when claiming the remittance basis on their annual Self-Assessment Tax Return.

The annual £30,000 charge:

- is payable in addition to Income Tax due on income remitted to the UK;

- is not itself taxed as a remittance if paid directly from an offshore source to HMRC.

Furthermore the unremitted income or gains on which the £30,000 tax is paid will not be taxed again if and when remitted to the UK.

Taxpayers who can claim the remittance basis do not have to do so. Then:

- they will then be taxed in the same way as other UK residents on income and gains arising in the tax year;

- tax will be payable on their worldwide income and gains for that tax year;

- they will be able to claim a personal allowance and the annual exempt limit on capital gains;

- they will need to complete a Self Assessment Tax Return in order to report any foreign income and gains for that tax year.

Individuals entitled to claim the remittance basis can decide from year to year whether they want to do so. In one year an individual might choose to pay the annual £30,000 charge and lose their allowances while in the next year opt to pay tax on all of their worldwide income and gains.

13   CAPITAL GAINS

The profits you make on disposing of your assets are known as capital gains and are subject to Capital Gains Tax. However, not all capital receipts are taxable. These include lottery, pools or gambling winnings, mortgage cash-backs and personal or professional damages. Profits made on disposing of the following types of asset are also tax free:

- private cars;
- National Savings;
- your home;
- chattels sold for less than £6,000;
- British Government securities and many corporate bonds;
- shares issued under the Enterprise Investment Scheme as long as the income tax relief has not been withdrawn;
- shares in Venture Capital Trusts;
- investments in an Individual Savings Account (ISA);
- gifts to charities or for the public benefit; and
- qualifying life policies on your life.

Taxable gains

This list includes profits you realize from disposing of:

- property;
- shares and unit trust investments;
- chattels sold for more than £6,000; and
- foreign currency other than that for personal use.

For Capital Gains Tax purposes, the date when the contract for purchase or sale is made determines the date when an asset is acquired or sold.

Tax payable

Every tax year you can make gains up to the annual exemption limit without paying tax. For 2010/11 the tax-free allowance is £10,100. Chargeable gains over and above this limit are taxed as follows:

- at the flat rate of 18% on gains made before 23 June 2010; or

- at flat rates of either 18% or 28% on gains realised on or after 23 June 2010. This is because the rate at which you pay is found by adding the gains to your taxable income.

As a result:

- The 28% rate will always apply if any part of your income bears tax above the basic rate.

- Tax at 18% will be payable if both your income and gains above the annual exemption limit together do not exceed the basic rate limit – £37,400 for 2010/11.

- Where your gains when added to your income exceed the basic rate limit you will pay tax at:

  — 18% on the amount of the gains within the basic rate band; and

  — 28% on the excess.

Isaac Woolf realised gains of £18,000, all after 23 June 2010, during 2010/11. His taxable income, after personal allowances and reliefs, was £34,000. The Capital Gains Tax he owes for the year is £1,872 as follows:

	£
Realized gains	18,000
Less: Exemption limit	10,100
	£7,900
Tax payable	
£3,400 @ 18%	612
£4,500 @ 28%	1,260
	£1,872

The amount of Capital Gains Tax @ 18% is worked out on the difference between the £37,400 limit of income taxable at the basic rate and Isaac's income of £34,000.

Where gains are subject to Capital Gains Tax at different rates you can deduct both:

- allowable losses; and
- the annual exemption limit

in the most beneficial way for you.

Michael Carver, who is a higher rate taxpayer, made gains and losses of £6,000 and £10,000 respectively in 2010/11, but before 23 June 2010. In the remainder of the tax year he realised gains of £28,000. The Capital Gains Tax he owes for the year is £3,292 as follows:

	£	£
On pre 23 June 2010 gains		
£6,000 @ 18%		1,080
On post 22 June 2010 gains		
Realized gains		28,000
Less: Losses in the year	10,000	
Annual Exemption Limit	10,100	
	------	20,100
		£7,900
Capital Gains Tax @ 28%		£2,212

Although Michael's losses arose before 23 June 2010 he can set these, as well as his full exemption limit for the year, against the gains he made after 22 June 2010.

Husband and wife

Husband and wife are:

- separately entitled to the annual exemption limit; and
- individually taxed on chargeable gains they realize in a tax year in excess of the annual exemption limit.

A married couple living together can transfer assets between them without gain or loss as follows:

- the recipient spouse is deemed to have acquired such assets at the cost to the former spouse;

- this exemption ceases when a couple permanently separate.

It is not uncommon for a married couple to own assets in their joint names. For tax purposes, a profit on disposal of a jointly owned asset is apportioned between husband and wife in the ratio of their respective interests in that asset at the date of disposal.

These rules extend to civil partners.

Working out chargeable gains

In calculating the taxable gain on the disposal of a chargeable asset, you are allowed to make certain deductions from the proceeds of sale as follows:

- the purchase price;

- incidental costs incurred on acquiring the asset;

- any additional expenditure you have incurred on enhancing the value of the asset, such as improvements or alterations to a property, during your period of ownership; and

- the costs of sale.

The list of incidental expenses which are allowed as either purchase or sale costs includes:

- solicitor's fees, including transfer and conveyancing costs;

- surveyor's, valuer's or auctioneer's fees;

- broker's commission;

- estate agent's commission, including advertising expenses;

- Stamp Duty Land Tax; and

- valuation costs.

Relief for losses

Losses and gains made in the same tax year are offset against each other. Any excess losses can be carried forward, without time limit, to reduce gains in subsequent tax years. But losses can never reduce the amount of your gains to below the annual exemption limit.

Bernard Levy had unused capital losses of £8,100 at 5 April 2010. During 2010/11 he made gains of £23,700 and incurred losses of £10,800.

His capital gains position for the year is:

	£	£
Gains realized in the year		23,700
Less: Losses — in the year	10,800	
— brought forward (part)	2,800	
	—–––	13,600
2010/11 Exemption limit		£10,100

The unused losses at 5 April 2011 of £5,300 can be carried forward to be set against gains in later years.

A loss:

- Arising on the sale or gift of an asset to a person with whom you are connected can only be set off against a gain on a similar disposal at a later date.

- Can be claimed where the value of an asset you own becomes negligible or nil. You do not actually have to dispose of the asset. The loss arises on the date that the relief is claimed. In practice, however, a two-year period is allowed from the end of the tax year in which the asset became of negligible value.

- On shares you subscribe for in a trading company not quoted on a recognized stock exchange can be set against your income, rather than against other capital gains. This applies whether you realize a loss on disposing of such shares or they become worthless.

Entrepreneurs' Relief

Entrepreneurs' Relief is a relief that can be claimed by individuals in working out their capital gains on the disposal of:

- all or part of a trading business carried on alone or in partnership;

- assets owned by an individual and used in their business;

- shares in an individual's own trading company;

- shares in a trading company where an individual is an employee or officer of the company and:

  — owns at least 5% of the company; or

  — has 5% or more of the voting rights.

The business, assets or shares, as the case may be, must be owned by the individual for at least a year prior to the date of disposal. However, on cessation a three year time limit is allowed in which to make the disposal providing the individual satisfied the one year requirement up to cessation.

Under Entrepreneurs' Relief:

- From 6 April 2010 to 22 June 2010:

  — the effective rate of Capital Gains Tax is reduced to 10%;

  — on your qualifying lifetime gains up to £2m;

  — the relief is given by reducing gains that qualify by 4/9ths.

- From 23 June 2010 to 5 April 2011:

  — the rate of Capital Gains Tax payable is 10%;

  — on your qualifying lifetime gains up to £5m.

Gains made on disposals before 6 April 2008 do not count towards the lifetime allowance.

In November 2010 Martin Osborne sold the shares he owned in his own trading company for £460,000. He originally bought the company in 1994 for £190,000. This was his only disposal in 2010/11. Martin pays Capital Gains Tax for the year of £25,990 as follows:

	£
Proceeds of sale	460,000
Less: Purchase price	190,000
Gain qualifying for Entrepreneurs' Relief	270,000
Less: Annual exemption limit	10,100
Gain chargeable to tax	£259,900
2010/11 Capital Gains Tax at 10%	£25,990

Assets owned on 31 March 1982

Gains and losses on disposals of assets that you held on 31 March 1982 must be calculated solely by reference to their market value at that date, ignoring original costs.

Ashley Barker acquired a freehold factory in the late 1970s for £25,000. It was valued at £30,000 on 31 March 1982. Ashley sold the factory in May 2010 for £120,000, after expenses of sale.

The chargeable gain is £90,000 as follows:

	£
Sale price	120,000
Less: March 1982 value	30,000
2010/11 chargeable gain	£90,000

Investments in shares

Before 6 April 1982 each shareholding was considered as a single asset and known as a 'pool' of shares. Every purchase of the same class of shares, or a sale of the part of the holding, represented either an addition to, or a disposal out of, the 'pool'. This changed when the indexation allowance was introduced. From 6 April 1982 each shareholding acquired was considered to be a separate asset. A further purchase of shares of a holding owned by you at 5 April 1982 could not be added to the 'pool'.

The rules were amended from 6 April 1985. Shares of the same class were again treated as a single asset growing or diminishing on each acquisition or disposal. This form of 'pooling' applied to shares acquired after 5 April 1982 unless they had already been disposed of before 6 April 1985. It is called a 'new holding'.

A 'pool' which was frozen under the 1982 rules had to stay that way. It continued as a single asset which could not grow by subsequent acquisitions and was known as a '1982 holding'.

A '1982 holding' is treated like any other asset in working out entitlement to the indexation allowance. This is not so for a 'new holding'. It had to be continuously indexed each time there was an addition to, or a disposal out of, the 'pool' up until April 1998.

All forms of 'pooling' ceased for shares acquired on or after 6 April 1998. This was when indexation was discontinued and replaced by taper relief. From that date until 5 April 2008 it was necessary to record and retain the date of acquisition of each holding of shares.

During this ten-year period the procedure for matching shares sold with their corresponding acquisition was as follows:

- shares acquired on the same day;

- shares acquired within 30 days following a disposal;

- shares acquired before the disposal, but after 5 April 1998, identifying the most recent acquisitions first;

- shares comprised in a 'new holding', the 1982–98 share pool;

- shares within a '1982 holding', the 1965–82 share pool;

- any shares acquired before 6 April 1965, last in first out; or

- shares acquired more than 30 days after the disposal.

Beginning with the 2008/09 tax year:

- following the withdrawal of both indexation and taper relief; and

- having to use the 31 March 1982 value, without exception, in working out capital gains and losses on disposals of assets acquired before that date,

a simplified set of identification rules have been introduced.

In the following order for shares of the same class which you own, these are:

- shares acquired on the same day;

- shares acquired within 30 days following a disposal;

- shares in 'a pool', no matter when they were acquired, which grows or diminishes whenever any shares are acquired or disposed of.

Laurence Stone made the following purchases in the shares of a quoted company:

Date	No of shares	Cost
1 June 1978	3,000	£4,500
1 November 1987	3,500	£7,000
1 November 1994	1,500	£5,000
13 August 2010	4,000	£12,000

During 2010/11 he also made the following sales:

Date	No of shares	Sale Proceeds
8 September 2010	2,000	£6,600
3 February 2011	6,000	£21,600

The shares were valued at £1.75 on 31 March 1982.

The 2,000 shares sold on 8 September 2010 must first of all, be identified with part of the acquisition of 4,000 shares on 13 August 2010 as follows:

	£
Proceeds of sale	6,600
Less: cost of 2,000 shares on 13 August 2010	6,000
Chargeable gain	£600

The sale of 6,000 shares on 3 February 2011 must be matched with the same number of shares in 'the pool' as follows:

£

	No of shares	Cost/Valuation
Shares acquired on 1 June 1978		
(at 31 March 1982 valuation)	3,000	5,250
Purchase in November 1987	3,500	7,000
Additional acquisition 1 September 1994	1,500	5,000
Purchase on 13 August 2010 (remainder)	2,000	6,000
	10,000	£23,250

	£
Proceeds of Sale of 6,000 shares on 3 February 2011	21,600
Less: deductible cost/value 6000/10,000 x £23,250	13,950
Chargeable gain	£7,650

The 'pool' of the remaining 4,000 shares, with a deductible cost/valuation of £9,300, is carried forward to future years.

The total chargeable gain on Laurence's two sales in 2010/11 is £8,250.

Whenever you receive a free or bonus issue of shares of the same class as an existing holding the date of their acquisition is the same as that of the original holding. The same principle applies to further shares acquired under a rights issue.

Where a company in which you have a holding is taken over and you receive:

- shares in the new company in exchange for your shares in the company taken over, no disposal for tax purposes takes place at that time. Your new holding is regarded as having being acquired at the same time, and for the same price, as the old one; or

- a mixture of cash and shares in the new company, a gain or a loss arises on the cash element of the takeover. It is then necessary to apportion the cost price of the old shares between the cash received and the value of the shareholding in the new company at the time.

Your home

The profit on the sale of your home is free of tax. The exemption automatically covers the house and the garden or grounds up to half a hectare, including the land on which the house is built. A larger area can qualify for exemption where it can be shown that it was required for the enjoyment of the house.

Where a home has not been lived in as your private residence throughout the full period of ownership or, if later, since 31 March 1982, a proportion of the gain on sale is taxable. Certain periods of absence are, however, disregarded in determining whether the gain is totally tax free. These are:

- the last three years of ownership always; and

- generally when you have to live away from home because of your work.

Guy Robinson sold his home in February 2011, making a profit of £90,000 as worked out for Capital Gains Tax purposes. He had bought the property in November 2004.

His job had taken him abroad between March 2005 and May 2007. Shortly after his return he bought a new home and moved there in August 2007.

The time spent working abroad and the last 36 months from February 2008 are also considered periods when the property was Guy's main residence. The chargeable gain is, therefore, restricted to the part of the gain apportioned to the six months between August 2007 and February 2008 as follows:

$$\frac{\text{Chargeable period}}{\text{Period of ownership}} = \frac{6 \text{ months}}{75 \text{ months}} \times £90,000 = \qquad £7,200$$

Where part of your home is used exclusively for business purposes, such as a surgery or office, the proportion of the profit on sale attributable to the business use:

- is a chargeable gain; and

- qualifies for the new Entrepreneurs' Relief.

If, during your period of ownership, a property is partly lived in as your home and rented out for the remainder of the time, the gain attributable to the period of letting which is exempt is the lower of:

- either £40,000; or

- an amount equivalent to the gain on the part you have occupied as your home.

Harriet Underwood made a taxable profit of £85,000 when she sold her flat in May 2010. She had acquired the property in April 2003 but only lived there from April 2007 until it was sold. For the remainder of the time the property was rented out. The chargeable gain is only £11,000 as follows:

		£	£
Capital gain (period of ownership			
– 85 months)			85,000
Less: Main residence exemption			
– 37 months		37,000	
Letting exemption – 48 months			
(lower of £40,000 or £37,000)		37,000	
			74,000
Chargeable gain			£11,000

A second home

It is not uncommon these days for individuals to have two properties. The main home is usually a house or flat within a commutable distance from the office or other place of work. The second property might be in the country, by the seaside or abroad in a warmer climate.

It is only the profit on the sale of your main residence which is tax free. Which one of your two or more homes is considered your main residence is usually a matter of fact. It is, however, possible for you to determine this in writing to your Tax Office. In the election you should state which of your homes you want regarded as your principal private residence for Capital Gains Tax purposes. The election can:

- commence from the date when you first have at least two homes available to you; or

- apply from any time in the two years starting with the commencement date;

- be made retrospectively on any date within two years of the commencement date; or

- be varied as and when it suits you.

Husband and wife living together are only allowed one qualifying home between them. The same applies to civil partners.

Pradeep and Sonia Singh bought their first home in January 2005 for £120,000. Not long afterwards Sonia received an inheritance from her father's estate and, with some of the money, they decided to buy a small flat by the seaside. This cost them £70,000 in October 2006. They elected for their first home to be their principal private residence for Capital Gains Tax purposes. In March 2011 they sold their holiday flat for £150,000, realizing a profit of £80,000. In order to reduce their tax bill they changed their main residence election to the holiday flat for the final four weeks up to the date of sale. The taxable gain, split equally between them, is £25,660 as follows:

	£
Profit on sale	80,000
Less: Main residence relief (last 3 years)	
$\dfrac{36 \text{ months}}{53 \text{ months}} \times £80,000$	54,340
Chargeable gain	£25,660

If you own a home which was occupied rent-free by the same dependant relative both on 5 April 1988 and throughout your period of ownership, then the profit on the sale is tax free.

Chattels

Profits from selling chattels with an expected life of more than 50 years and which are sold for less than £6,000 are tax free. Chattels include paintings and other works of art, antiques, furniture, jewellery, stamps and ornaments. Articles comprising a set are considered as a single item when they are sold to the same person but at different times.

For items which fetch between £6,000 and £15,000, the chargeable gain is restricted to 5/3 times the amount by which the proceeds of sale (ignoring expenses) exceeds £6,000 where this is to your advantage.

Meryl Nichols sold an antique vase at auction in March 2011 for £10,500, receiving £9,750 after expenses of sale.

She had inherited the vase from her mother when she died in April 1987. It was then valued at only £1,000.

The chargeable gain is £7,500 as follows:

	£
Net sale price	9,750
Less: Acquisition cost	1,000
Profit	£8,750
But restricted to $5/3$ x £4,500 (£10,500 – £6,000)	£7,500

When an article is sold for under £6,000 and at a loss, the allowable loss is restricted by assuming the sale proceeds were equal to £6,000.

Vincent Wells bought a set of stamps in the late 1980s for £8,300. The set was sold in December 2010 for £6,600. Vincent's allowable loss is £1,700. If he had only made £3,800 on the sale, the tax loss would have been £2,300 (£8,300 – £6,000).

Gifts and valuations

There are times when a figure different from the actual disposal proceeds is used in the calculation of a capital gain. This happens, for example, when you make a gift or sell an asset at a nominal value to a close member of your family. On these occasions you must work out the capital gain based on the open-market value of the asset at the time of gift or disposal.

Whenever you need to use valuations to work out the gain or loss in such circumstances, there is a free service from HMRC which will help you complete your Self-Assessment Tax Return.

You may ask your Tax Office to check valuations after you have made the disposal but before you make your return:

- you can ask for one copy of form CG34 for each valuation you want confirmed; and

- you must then return the completed form to your Tax Office together with all the other information and documents requested on the form.

Agreed valuations will not subsequently be challenged when you submit your Tax Return unless you did not previously mention important facts affecting the valuations. If your figures are not agreed, HMRC will put forward alternative valuations.

Where the gift is one of a business asset, you can elect jointly with the transferee for payment of the tax on the gift to be postponed until the asset is subsequently disposed of by the transferee.

Short life assets

Short life, or wasting, assets are those with an expected lifespan of less than 50 years. A gain on the disposal of a wasting asset is worked out in the same way as that on the disposal of any other asset, except that the purchase price wastes away during the expected lifespan of the asset.

Leases of land for less than 50 years are wasting assets. There is a specific formula for calculating the proportion of the purchase price of a lease that can be deducted from the sale proceeds.

The gain or loss on the sale of a wasting asset that is also 'tangible moveable property' is outside of tax.

Part disposals

Where you dispose of only part of an asset that you own:

- You apportion the acquisition cost between the part sold and the fraction retained. This is worked out on a pro-rata basis by reference to the sale proceeds of the part sold and the open-market value of the proportion retained.

- The proportion of cost price of the asset attributable to the part retained can be set against the proceeds on the sale of the remainder at a later date.

- If the part sold is small compared with the value of the whole asset you can simply deduct the sale proceeds from the acquisition cost. Where the part disposal is one of land this procedure can be followed so long as the sale proceeds are both less than £20,000 and one-fifth of the value of the remaining land.

Enterprise Investment Scheme

A profit on disposing of qualifying shares under the Enterprise Investment Scheme (EIS) is free of Capital Gains Tax, provided:

- the Income Tax relief originally allowed on the investment has not been withdrawn; and

- the disposal takes place at least three years after the issue of the shares.

If you incur a loss on disposing of qualifying shares you can offset the loss against either:

- capital gains in the same year that the loss is realized; or

- your taxable income in the year of loss, or the previous year.

It is also possible to defer Capital Gains Tax payable on chargeable gains by reinvesting the gains in qualifying EIS shares. For deferral relief purposes the chargeable gains must be reinvested in the period beginning one year before, and ending three years after, the original disposal. Deferral relief can be claimed:

- along with both Income Tax relief (see Chapter 10) and exemption from Capital Gains Tax (as above) up to an annual investment limit of £500,000; or

- on its own as the amount of gains that can be deferred is unlimited; or

- in any other combination you choose within the rules.

If deferral relief is claimed the original liability to Capital Gains Tax will crystallize when the EIS shares are sold.

Venture Capital Trusts

A disposal of shares in a Venture Capital Trust (VCT) is exempt from Capital Gains Tax provided:

- the original subscription for the shares disposed of did not exceed the maximum permitted investment limit in the year of purchase, £200,000 for 2010/11; and

- the company qualifies as a VCT both at the time the shares are acquired and at the date of disposal.

Inheritances

No Capital Gains Tax is payable on the unrealized profits on your assets as at the date of your death. When you inherit an asset you acquire it at the value on the date of death of the deceased. Generally, this rule is also applied whenever you become entitled to assets from a Trust.

14 HOW TO COMPLETE YOUR TAX RETURN AND WORK OUT YOUR TAX

This tax guide is being published shortly after HMRC have sent out Tax Returns:

- requiring taxpayers, by law, to make a Return of their taxable income and capital gains for the year from 6 April 2010 to 5 April 2011; and

- enabling them to claim the allowances and tax reliefs to which they are entitled for the same year.

Do I need to complete a Tax Return?

If:

- your tax affairs are not complicated; and

- you receive income taxed under PAYE

you probably don't need to complete a Tax Return.

But:

- if your tax affairs are not straightforward; and

- you receive income from several sources

you may need to fill one in.

Who has to complete a Tax Return?

HMRC will want a Tax Return from you each year if you:

- are self-employed;

- are a company director;

- own land or property in the UK from which you receive rents;

- have other untaxed income and it is not possible to collect the tax due through your PAYE Tax Code;

- make capital gains in excess of the annual exemption limit; or

- are an employee or pensioner with more complex tax affairs.

Employees and pensioners with complex tax affairs

You must fill in a Tax Return if you:

- have an annual income of at least £100,000;

- receive income from savings or investments of at least £10,000 (before tax) in a year;

- have untaxed income in excess of £2,500; or

- owe tax at the end of the year which cannot be collected in the following year through your PAYE Tax Code.

The Tax Return

The Tax Return runs to six pages. In the same envelope from HMRC you will also find:

- a separate four page section of Additional Information pages for dealing with the less common types of income and tax reliefs;

- a Tax Return Guide;

- supplementary colour-coded pages based on your tax history.

The list of the various supplementary pages is as follows:

Employment	Pink
Self-employment	Orange
Partnership	Turquoise
UK property	Red
Foreign	Mustard
Trusts etc	Brown
Capital Gains Summary	Blue
Residence, remittance basis etc	Green

Getting started

When your Return arrives try to avoid the temptation of putting it to one side. It is better to get on with the job of filling in the Return as soon as you can because you will:

- have more time to get help from HMRC if you need it;

- have more time to save for any tax you owe;

- find out earlier if you are due a tax refund; and

- get a big weight off your mind!!

Start by going to page TR2. This will help you decide which, if any, supplementary pages you need. These can be obtained by:

- telephoning the Orderline on 0845 9000 404 (open seven days a week from 8 a.m. to 10 p.m.); or

- going to www.hmrc.gov.uk to download them.

The supplementary pages come with Notes to help you fill in the pages you requested. Help sheets which may also further assist you in working out the income or capital gains to be declared on these supplementary pages will be mentioned in the Notes and are similarly available from HMRC.

Filing deadline – paper

If you decide to complete a paper Tax Return for 2010/11 you must send it back by 31 October 2011 so HMRC has time:

- to work out the tax you owe or the refund due to you; and

- let you know the result of their calculation before the 31 January 2012 payment deadline.

If HMRC receive your paper 2010/11 Tax Return by 31 October 2011 and you:

- owe tax of not more than £2,000; and

- have a PAYE tax code,

they will, if possible, collect the tax you owe for the year through next year's tax code unless your preference is to make direct payment by 31 January 2012.

Filing deadline – online

The deadline for filing your 2010/11 Return online is 31 January 2012 so if, for example, you miss the 31 October 2011 time limit for paper filing you can still file your Return online by 31 January 2012. HMRC is strongly recommending and encouraging taxpayers to file online because:

- it is secure and convenient;

- tax calculations are done for you automatically;

- on-screen help is available if you need it;

- you get an immediate acknowledgement that your Return has been received; and

- if you are owed money, you will get a faster repayment.

You can also:

- see whether HMRC owe you money, or how much you owe HMRC;

- view your statement of account for the last three years;

- make changes to your personal contact details;

- make a claim to reduce payments on account or request a refund (if your account is in credit).

To file online go to www.hmrc.gov.uk and from the 'do it online' menu on the left of the screen select 'Self-Assessment'.

Keeping proper records

Before you come to complete the rest of your Tax Return you need to gather together all the information on your income, capital gains, reliefs and allowances from the records you have been keeping for the year to 5 April 2011. For most types of income and capital gains you only need to retain the records given to you by whoever provided that income or realized the gains for you. This means for those of you,

- in employment:
  — your Form P60, a certificate your employer will give you after 5 April (the end of the tax year) detailing your pay and the tax deducted from it;
  — Form P11D or P9D or equivalent information from your employer showing any benefits-in-kind and expenses payments you received;

— any Form P45 (part 1A) certificate from an employer showing pay and tax from a job you have left;

— any Form P160 (part 1A) you may have been given when you retire and then go on to receive a pension from your former employer;

— your payslips or pay statements;

— a note of the amount of any tips or gratuities along with details of any other taxable receipts. You are well advised to note these as soon as possible after you receive them, and not simply estimate them at the end of the year.

- receiving a UK pension or social security benefits:

— your Form P60, a certificate given to you by the payer of your occupational pension, stating the amount of your pension and the tax deducted;

— a certificate detailing any other pension you received and the tax deducted from it;

— information given to you by the Department of Work and Pensions (DWP) relating to state pensions, taxable state benefits, statutory sick, maternity or paternity pay and the jobseekers allowance.

- in business or letting property:

— this is dealt with in the section on records in Chapter 7.

- receiving investment income:

— bank and building society statements, passbooks and tax deduction certificates;

— statements of interest and any other income received from your savings and investments; for example, an annuity;

— vouchers for dividends received from UK companies;

— unit trust tax vouchers;

— life insurance chargeable event certificates;

— details of any income you received from a trust or the estate of a deceased person;

— information about any exceptional amounts – such as an inheritance or other windfall – which you receive and subsequently invest.

- making capital gains or losses:

— contracts for the purchase or sale of shares, unit trusts, property or any other assets;

— copies of any valuations you need to work out your capital gains or losses;

— bills, invoices or other evidence of payment records such as bank statements and cheque stubs for costs you claim for the purchase, improvement or sale of assets;

— details of any assets you have given away or put into a trust.

• claiming personal allowances, other deductions or reliefs:

— certificates of interest paid on any loans which qualify for tax relief;

— declarations you have made to charities of gifts under Gift Aid;

— receipts for the payment of pension premiums;

— notification that you are registered as a blind person.

This list of the types of records you are advised to keep is not exhaustive and does not cover every situation. If you are in any doubt, ask your tax office or Tax Enquiry Centre for assistance.

The period for which you must keep your records is:

• the fifth anniversary of 31 January following the tax year if you are self-employed, in partnership or letting property;

• in any other case the first 31 January anniversary after the tax year.

Filling in your Tax Return

The Tax Return is designed to be read by a machine. It is important to complete the form properly so that it is correctly read.

Always:

• use black ink and capital letters;

• cross out any mistakes and write the correct information below;

• enter figures in whole pounds, ignoring pence;

• round down income;

• round up expenses and tax paid – this will benefit you;

• if a box does not apply simply leave it blank.

There is not enough space for me to reproduce the six page Tax Return, as well as the Additional Information and supplementary pages. In the following pages you will find reproductions of the supplementary page on Employment, most of the sections for the Tax Return and some of those from the Additional Information pages.

If you have more than one job you will need to fill in a separate employment page for each job as follows:

- in box 1 enter your before-tax salary or wage from your P60 or P45;

- enter the tax taken off your pay in box 2;

- tips and other payments not on your P60 go in box 3;

- the PAYE tax reference of your employer, which will be shown on your P60 or P45, needs to be entered in box 4;

- box 5 is for your employer's name;

- use your Form P11D, or equivalent information, to enter the taxable amounts of any benefits from your employment in boxes 9 to 16; and

- any business travel or subsistence expenses, professional fees and subscriptions and other expenses paid by you and on which you can claim tax relief go in boxes 17 to 20.

HM Revenue & Customs

Employment

Tax year 6 April 2010 to 5 April 2011

Your name

Simon Black

Your Unique Taxpayer Reference (UTR)

4 3 2 9 6   5 5 4 3 4

Complete an *Employment* page for each employment or directorship

1 Pay from this employment - the total from your P45 or P60 - *before tax was taken off*

£ **2 6 5 2 0** · 0 0

2 UK tax taken off pay in box 1

£ **5 1 2 0** · 0 0

3 Tips and other payments not on your P60 - *read page EN 3 of the notes*

£ · 0 0

4 PAYE tax reference of your employer (on your P45/P60)

2 8 / B 6 0 4

5 Your employer's name

**B R O A D W O O D
E N G I N E E R S   L T D**

6 If you were a company director, put 'X' in the box

7 And, if the company was a close company, put 'X' in the box

8 If you are a part-time teacher in England or Wales and are on the Repayment of Teachers' Loans Scheme for this employment, put 'X' in the box

Benefits from your employment - use your form P11D (or equivalent information)

9 Company cars and vans - *the total 'cash equivalent' amount*

£ **1 8 0 0** · 0 0

10 Fuel for company cars and vans - *the total 'cash equivalent' amount*

£ **2 8 7 3** · 0 0

11 Private medical and dental insurance - *the total 'cash equivalent' amount*

£ **5 0 0** · 0 0

12 Vouchers, credit cards and excess mileage allowance

£ · 0 0

13 Goods and other assets provided by your employer - *the total value or amount*

£ · 0 0

14 Accommodation provided by your employer - *the total value or amount*

£ · 0 0

15 Other benefits (including interest-free and low interest loans) - *the total 'cash equivalent' amount*

£ · 0 0

16 Expenses payments received and balancing charges

£ · 0 0

Employment expenses

17 Business travel and subsistence expenses

£ · 0 0

18 Fixed deductions for expenses

£ · 0 0

19 Professional fees and subscriptions

£ · 0 0

20 Other expenses and capital allowances

£ · 0 0

ℹ **Shares schemes, employment lump sums, compensation, deductions and Seafarers' Earnings Deduction** are on the *Additional information* pages enclosed in the tax return pack

Leaving aside the sections on the first two pages of the Tax Return asking for your personal details and repayments of student loans the first part of page TR3 is for you to report your income from UK interest and dividends as follows:

- in box 1 you should enter the total of the net amount after tax of the interest on all your bank, building society and other interest bearing accounts;

- you may have received interest where no tax has been taken off at source. If so this is the figure to enter in box 2;

- dividend cheques on your shareholdings come with counterfoils. These show the amount of the dividend and the accompanying tax credit. It is only the total of all your dividends in the year, excluding tax credits, which should be entered in box 3;

- you should do likewise in completing box 4 in respect of any dividends received from authorised unit trusts and open-ended investment companies;

- boxes 5 and 6 are for your foreign dividends, up to £300, and the tax taken off these foreign dividends.

Interest and dividends from UK banks, building societies etc.

1 Taxed UK interest etc. - *the net amount after tax has been taken off (see notes)* £ 8 0 0 · 0 0	4 Other dividends - *do not include the tax credit (see notes)* £ 3 1 5 · 0 0
2 Untaxed UK interest etc. - *amounts which have not been taxed (see notes)* £ 3 4 0 · 0 0	5 Foreign dividends (up to £300) - *the amount in sterling after foreign tax was taken off. Do not include this amount in the Foreign pages* £ 1 0 0 · 0 0
3 Dividends from UK companies - *do not include the tax credit (see notes)* £ 8 1 0 · 0 0	6 Tax taken off foreign dividends - *the sterling equivalent* £ 1 5 · 0 0

The next section on page TR3 deals with UK pensions, annuities and other State benefits received as follows:

- the figure to put in box 7 is the total of your weekly entitlements to the State Pension, even if you were paid monthly or quarterly. If you do not know the figure telephone Pensions Direct on 0845 301 3011 and ask for a Form BR735 for the year from 6 April 2010 to 5 April 2011. Do not include either the Christmas bonus or your winter fuel payment as these are not taxable;

- you will only need to complete boxes 8 and 9 if you received a State Pension lump sum in the year;

- all your other pension income, and the tax taken off, needs to be shown in boxes 10 and 11. In box 19 on page 6 you should separately list the names of the payers of your pensions, the amounts paid and the tax deducted;

- the remaining boxes are relevant if you are receiving incapacity benefit, other State Pensions or benefits which are taxable.

UK pensions, annuities and other state benefits received

7 State Pension - *the amount due for the year (see notes)*

5 0 7 7 ·

8 State Pension lump sum

9 Tax taken off box 8

10 Pensions (other than State Pension), retirement annuities and taxable triviality payments - *give details of the payers. amounts paid and tax deducted in the 'Any other information' box, box 19, on page TR 6*

1 6 5 0 0 ·

11 Tax taken off box 10

2 4 1 8 ·

12 Taxable Incapacity Benefit and contribution-based Employment and Support Allowance - *see notes*

13 Tax taken off Incapacity Benefit in box 12

14 Jobseeker's Allowance

15 Total of any other taxable State Pensions and benefits

The final section on page TR3 is for reporting other UK income not included on the supplementary pages and, in most cases, is unlikely to be relevant to your circumstances.

Page TR4 is primarily devoted to tax reliefs, the first part of which is relevant if you want to claim relief for pension contributions. It is likely that the only boxes you are likely to complete are Nos. 1 and 2.

Paying into registered pension schemes and overseas pension schemes

Do not include payments you make to your employer's pension scheme which are deducted from your pay before tax or payments made by your employer.

1 Payments to registered pension schemes where basic rate tax relief will be claimed by your pension provider (called 'relief at source'). Enter the payments and basic rate tax

4 0 0 0 ·

2 Payments to a retirement annuity contract where basic rate tax relief will not be claimed by your provider

2 6 0 0 ·

3 Payments to your employer's scheme which were not deducted from your pay before tax

4 Payments to an overseas pension scheme which is not UK-registered which are eligible for tax relief and were not deducted from your pay before tax

If you pay tax at the higher or additional rates you will be entitled to tax relief on the difference between either 40% or 50% and the basic rate of 20% on your donations to charities under Gift Aid. However, even if you are not claiming this tax relief you should complete the part of the Return on charitable giving as follows:

- the total of all your Gift Aid payments goes in box 5;

- in box 6 you need to enter the total of any 'one-off' payments in the figure in box 5;

- any Gift Aid donations made in 2010/11 and related back to 2009/10 go in box 7;

- perhaps by the time you fill in your Tax Return and send it back to your tax office you have made donations under Gift Aid in the 2011/12 tax year. You can elect to have those payments treated as though they were made in the year to 5 April 2011. Enter the figure in box 8;

- the value of any shares or securities, land and buildings which you have gifted to charity in the year should be entered in boxes 9 and 10 respectively.

In boxes 11 and 12 you should respectively state:

- the value of any investments gifted to non-UK charities in boxes 9 and 10; and

- Gift Aid payments to non-UK charities in box 5.

Charitable giving

5 Gift Aid payments made in the year to 5 April 2011	9 Value of qualifying shares or securities gifted to charity
1 6 0 0 ·	5 0 0 0 ·
6 Total of any 'one-off' payments in box 5	10 Value of qualifying land and buildings gifted to charity
1 1 0 0 ·	· 0 0
7 Gift Aid payments made in the year to 5 April 2011 but treated as if made in the year to 5 April 2010	11 Value of qualifying investments gifted to non-UK charities in boxes 9 and 10
7 0 0 ·	2 0 0 ·
8 Gift Aid payments made after 5 April 2011 but to be treated as if made in the year to 5 April 2011	12 Gift Aid payments to non-UK charities in box 5
9 0 0 ·	· 0 0

The next tax relief section on page TR4 is only of relevance to you if you can make a claim for the special blind persons allowance. You need to give the name of the local authority, or equivalent body, with whom you have registered your blindness.

Blind Person's Allowance

13 If you are registered blind on a local authority or other register, put 'X' in the box **X**	15 If you want your spouse's, or civil partner's, surplus allowance, put 'X' in the box
14 Enter the name of the local authority or other register **TOPMARSH COUNCIL**	16 If you want your spouse, or civil partner, to have your surplus allowance, put 'X' in the box

Pages TR5 and TR6 are all about finishing off your Tax Return. However, before you do so, you may need to complete some of the sections on the Additional Information pages which are for less common types of income, deductions and tax reliefs, and for other information. The second section on page Ai2 is for you to claim other tax reliefs, such as:

- your subscriptions for new ordinary shares in a Venture Capital Trust in box 1;

- box 2 is for your subscriptions for shares issued under the Enterprise Investment Scheme;

- The total of your qualifying loan interest payable in the year should be entered in box 5;

- maintenance or alimony payments you are making, subject to a maximum of £2,670, should be entered in box 7 but only if you or your former spouse or civil partner was born before 6 April 1935.

Other tax reliefs

1 Subscriptions for Venture Capital Trust shares – *the amount on which relief is claimed* £ **6 0 0 0** · 0 0	6 Post-cessation expenses and certain other losses £ · 0 0
2 Subscriptions for shares under the Enterprise Investment Scheme – *the amount on which relief is claimed (and provide more information on page Ai 4)* £ **2 5 0 0** · 0 0	7 Maintenance payments (max £2,670) – *only if you or your former spouse or civil partner were born before 6 April 1935* £ **1 4 0 0** · 0 0
3 Community Investment Tax Relief – *the amount on which relief is claimed* £ · 0 0	8 Payments to a trade union etc. for death benefits – *half the amount paid (max £100)* £ · 0 0
4 UK royalties and annual payments made £ · 0 0	9 Relief claimed for employer's compulsory widow's, widower's or orphan's benefit scheme – *(max £20)* £ · 0 0
5 Qualifying loan interest payable in the year £ **1 7 3 0** · 0 0	10 Relief claimed on a qualifying distribution on the redemption of bonus shares or securities £ · 0 0

Then follows a section on the age related married couple's allowance. You should carefully read the notes at the top of page Ai3 before completing boxes 1 to 11 as appropriate.

Age-related Married Couple's Allowance

If you are the **husband** (marriages up to 5 December 2005), or the **spouse or civil partner, with the higher income** (marriages and civil partnerships on or after 5 December 2005) you should complete box 1 and, where appropriate, boxes 2 to 5 and box 9. If you want to claim or transfer surplus allowances, complete box 10 or box 11 as well.

If you are the **wife** (marriages up to 5 December 2005), or the **spouse or civil partner, with the lower income** (marriages and civil partnerships on or after 5 December 2005) please read the notes on page AiN 23. These notes will help you fill in boxes 6 to 11.

If you, or your spouse or civil partner, were born **before** 6 April 1935, complete the relevant boxes

1 Your spouse's or civil partner's full name

WENDY MARTIN

2 Their date of birth if older than you (and at least one of you was born before 6 April 1935) *DD MM YYYY*

25 09 1923

3 If you have already agreed that **half** the minimum allowance is to go to your spouse or civil partner, put 'X' in the box

X

4 If you have already agreed that **all** of the minimum allowance is to go to your spouse or civil partner, put 'X' in the box

5 If, in the year to 5 April 2011, you lived with any previous spouse or civil partner, enter their date of birth

6 If you have already agreed that **half** of the minimum allowance is to be given to you, put 'X' in the box

7 If you have already agreed that **all** of the minimum allowance is to be given to you, put 'X' in the box

8 Your spouse's or civil partner's full name

9 If you were married or formed a civil partnership after 5 April 2010, enter the date of marriage or civil partnership *DD MM YYYY*

10 If you want to have your spouse's or civil partner's surplus allowance, put 'X' in the box

11 If you want your spouse or civil partner to have your surplus allowance, put 'X' in the box

Now you can put the finishing touches to your Tax Return. If you want to calculate your tax you will have to ask HMRC for the Tax Calculation Summary pages and notes which will help you work out:

- any tax due or repayable; and

- if payments on account are necessary.

There is a choice of boxes to complete if you have not paid enough tax. But if you have overpaid you need to give the information requested in boxes 4 to 14 on page TR5 of the bank or building society account into which you would like the tax refund paid. This is both the safest and quickest method for HMRC to deal with any tax refund due to you.

Do not miss the deadline for filing your Tax Return because, perhaps, you are waiting for some final figures. Use estimates and make sure you send the correct figures as soon as you can. You should tick box 20 on page TR6 of your Return and describe in the space provided at box 19:

- which figures are provisional. You should refer to the appropriate box numbers on your Tax Return or any other supplementary pages you have completed;

- why you could not give final figures; and

- when you expect to be able to provide your tax office with the correct information.

Put 'X' in box 21 if you are enclosing separate supplementary pages. You must then sign and date the Return in box 22. Have regard to the wording of the declaration: 'the information I have given in this Return and any supplementary pages is correct and complete to the best of my knowledge and belief.' The form and any supplementary pages are now ready to send back to your tax office.

Working out your tax

The key steps in calculating your tax bill are as follows:

(1) add up all the non-savings income you have entered on your Return;

(2) total the allowances and other deductions you have claimed for the year but excluding those such as personal pension premiums and donations under Gift Aid paid net of tax at the basic rate;

(3) take (2) away from (1);

(4) work out the tax due on (3) but increasing the basic rate band of £37,400 by the grossed up equivalent of personal pension and Gift Aid payments;

(5) if you are taxable at the higher or additional rates of 40% and 50% work out the additional tax payable on your savings income and dividends;

(6) add (4) and (5) together;

(7) if you are self-employed or in partnership work out how much you owe for Class 4 National Insurance contributions; and

(8) add (6) and (7) together and take away all tax deducted at source.

This is your tax bill unless you also owe tax on capital gains realized in excess of your annual exemption limit. You will then be able to:

- work out what tax you have to pay for 2010/11 due on 31 January 2012;

- calculate any payments on account for 2011/12 payable on 31 January and 31 July 2012.

Illustration

Celia Mercer, who is single, is employed as a fashion designer. She frequently has to travel so her employer provides her with a company car, fuel for private mileage as well as private medical insurance cover.

In her spare time Celia speaks at trade shows. She also writes articles for fashion magazines.

A few years ago Celia's mother died. The inheritance she received is invested in a portfolio of shares. She also owns a buy-to-let flat and has spare cash deposited in building society accounts.

Celia filed her Tax Return for the year to 5 April 2011 on 20 October 2011. It shows the following entries:

		£	Page No.	Box No.
(1)	**Employment**			
	Salary	48,000	E1	1
	Tax deducted by employer	11,819	E1	2
	Company Car benefit	2,880	E1	9
	Car Fuel benefit	3,042	E1	10
	Medical insurance	800	E1	11
(2)	**Self-Employment**			
	Adjusted profit shown by the Accounts for the year to 30 September 2010	6,000	SEF4	75
(3)	**U.K. Property**			
	Net rental income from buy-to-let flat	4,500	UKP2	38
(4)	**U.K. Interest and Dividends**			
	Building Society interest	1,200	TR3	1
	Dividends from U.K. companies	1,620	TR3	2

	£	Page No.	Box No.
(5) Reliefs			
Personal pension premiums	2,200	TR4	1
Interest on loan to buy			
investment flat	3,100	Ai2	5
(6) Capital Gains			
In excess of annual			
exemption limit on profits			
made in October 2010	1,600	CG1	8

The calculation of Celia's tax liability for 2010/11 is as follows:

	£	£
Employment		
Salary	48,000	
Taxable benefits	5,922	
	————	53,922
Self-employment		6,000
Net rental income		4,500
		————
		64,422
Less: Personal allowance	6,475	
Interest on buy-to-let loan	3,100	
	————	9,575
		————
		£54,847
		═══════
Tax thereon:		
The first £37,400 @ 20%	7,480.00	
The next £2,200 @ 20%	440.00	
(the personal pension premiums)		
The balance of £15,247 @ 40%	6,098.80	
	————	14,018.80
Add: further tax on savings income		
Taxed interest (£1,200 × 100/80)		
@ 20%	300.00	
Dividends @ 25%	405.00	
	————	705.00
Add: Capital Gains Tax		
£1,600 @ 28%		448.00
		————
		15,171.80
Less: Tax deducted from salary		11,819.00
		————
Tax due for 2010/11		**£3,352.80**
		═══════

TAX PAYMENTS

Tax due for 2010/11 (as above)	3,352.80
Payment on account made 31 January 2011	(1,500.00)
Payment on account made 31 July 2011	(1,500.00)
Balance due for 2010/11	352.80
Add: First payment on account for 2011/12	1,596.40
Amount due on 31 January 2012	£1,949.20
Second payment on account for 2011/12	1,596.40
Amount due on 31 July 2012	£1,596.40

Notes:
(1) Celia applied for, and was granted, permission to defer payment of Class 4 National Insurance Contributions.
(2) Tax payments of £1,500 were made by Celia on both 31 January and 31 July 2011 based on her tax liability for 2009/10.

What HMRC does

When your completed Tax Return is received by your tax office it will be processed as quickly as possible based on your entries on the Return. Any simple straightforward mistakes will be corrected by HMRC and you will be told about them.

You will then be sent a calculation of your tax position if you have asked HMRC to work this out for you. Alternatively if you have calculated your own tax bill, and it is incorrect, HMRC will send you their tax calculation.

15 PAYING YOUR TAX, INTEREST, SURCHARGES AND PENALTIES

Under the Self-Assessment tax system:

- there are specified dates each year when you must pay your tax;

- you regularly receive a Statement of Account from HMRC detailing both tax recently paid and the next amount due.

Tax payment dates

The tax payment dates for 2010/11 are:

		Due Date for Tax Payments on Account	Due Date for Final Balance
Rental income and untaxed investment income			
Business profits	50%	31/01/2011	31/01/2012
Unpaid PAYE (where not coded)	50%	31/07/2011	
Higher and Additional Rate Tax on investment income (taxed at source)			
Capital Gains Tax		N/A	31/01/2012

The one exception to the rule requiring direct payment of tax to HMRC relates to employees or pensioners who owe less than £2,000 in tax. They can choose to have the amount collected monthly in the following year through the PAYE system:

- by filing a paper return at their Tax Office no later than 31 October following the end of the tax year; or

- by filing online by 30 December after the end of the tax year.

Payments on account

As the table on the previous page shows, some taxpayers, who will mainly be the self-employed, will make two payments on account of the tax due for a year on:

- 31 January in the tax year; and

- 31 July following the end of the tax year.

Payments on account are worked out by splitting into two equal amounts the tax paid for the previous tax year (after taking off tax incurred at source and any Capital Gains Tax).

You do not need to make payments on account of Income Tax if:

- the amount you owe for Income Tax and Class 4 National Insurance Contributions for the previous tax year – after taking off tax paid at source on, for example, dividends, bank and building society interest – is less than £1,000; or

- at least 80% of your Income Tax and Class 4 National Insurance Contributions bill for the preceding tax year was represented by tax deducted from the income before you received it.

It follows that most employees and pensioners will not have to make the half-yearly payments on account.

Reduced payments on account

Maybe, because of a change in your financial circumstances particularly in view of the present difficult economic climate, your payments on account for the tax year (based on what you paid in the previous year) point towards an overstatement of your likely liability for the year.

This might happen where you expect:

- your income in 2011/12 to be lower than that in 2010/11;

- your allowances or reliefs to be higher;

- that more of your income will incur tax at source in 2011/12, because:

  — it will be taxed under PAYE; or

  — your savings income taxed at source will increase.

In such circumstances you can claim to reduce your payments on account. You do this by using Form SA303, which is available at your Tax Office. The form gives guidance on how to complete it. When you have done this and signed it you should send it back to your Tax Office for processing.

If the claim to reduce your payments on account subsequently turns out to be excessive then you will be asked to pay interest on the difference between the reduced tax you actually paid and the payments on account that should have been made.

Business Payment Support Service

In response to the current economic conditions HMRC introduced a Business Support Service dedicated to assist businesses with temporary cash flow problems.

If you are concerned:

- about being able to meet tax, National Insurance or other payments due to HMRC; or

- that future payments could cause you difficulties,

you can get in touch with HMRC to discuss payment options.

You will be asked for the following information:

- your tax reference number;

- details of the tax that you are or will have trouble paying;

- an outline summary of the income and expenses of your business.

This will enable HMRC staff to review your particular circumstances and discuss temporary options relevant to the needs of your business which could, for example, include allowing you to make tax payments over a longer period. You will not be charged late payment surcharges in such an arrangement although interest will continue to accrue on payments made beyond their due and payable date.

The number to telephone if you need assistance is 0845 302 1435.

Statements of account

The main features of the statements sent to taxpayers showing their account with HMRC are:

- an opening balance, if any, brought forward from the previous statement;

- what has happened since the last statement;

- whether there is an over payment or, most probably, an amount to pay, and when to pay it.

If you are making payments on account you can expect to receive the following statements up to February 2012:

July 2011	**To tell you of the second payment on account for 2010/11 due on 31 July 2011.**
August 2011	**To let you know of any outstanding balance of the second payment on account. The statement will also include a figure for interest due to date.**
January 2012	**To advise you of your balancing payment for 2010/11 and your first payment on account for 2011/12, both due on this date.**
February 2012	**To show any outstanding amounts which should have been paid on 31 January 2012. The statement will also include a charge for interest due to date.**

You will also receive statements of account:

- whenever they are amended;

- every month where there is an outstanding amount in excess of £500;

- every two months where you still owe tax of between £32 and £500; and

- where you are due a refund from HMRC (but only once!).

Other points of interest are:

- As HMRC carry out security checks any tax refund due to you may not actually be issued until sometime after the date shown on your Statement of Account.

- Where a tax liability will shortly be due for payment HMRC will usually set any tax refund against this amount and then just repay the balance.

- If you have made a payment in the short period before you receive a Statement it will appear on the next one.

If you have registered for Self-Assessment Online you can access a wide range of services to include:

- viewing the latest issued copy of your Statement, as well as any Statements issued to you in the last three years;

- viewing payments/credits and how these have been allocated;

- viewing liabilities by tax year including interest, penalties and surcharges;

- requesting repayments where an account is in credit;

- claiming to reduce payments on account;

- viewing and changing your address; and

- paying by Direct Debit online.

Paying your tax

There are a number of secure and efficient methods for paying your tax recommended by HMRC. If you use payment by post you should make your cheque payable to 'HM Revenue and Customs only' followed by your Unique Taxpayer Reference. Your cheque should be accompanied by the tear-off payment slip from your statement of account and both of these should be sent, unfolded, in the envelope provided (postage is no longer pre-paid) or to HM Revenue and Customs, Accounts Office, Bradford, BD99 1YY.

HMRC politely requests that:

- you do not staple or attach paperclips to cheques; and

- you do not pay your tax by sending cash through the post.

You can assist your Accounts Office in dealing promptly with your tax payment by:

- including a separate letter if you are sending a post-dated cheque, or want to give further information about your payment; and

- paying on time – you will not then incur interest charges.

You can also pay:

- using the internet or telephone;

- at a post office or your bank;

- by debit card (Switch, Solo, Electron or Visa Delta) over the internet; or

- by direct debit. This service is available online. You have a choice of setting up either a Single Payment or a Budget Payment Plan.

Many of us:

- already use Direct Debit to make regular payments for household and other costs; and

- are familiar with the advantages of paying by Direct Debit.

Under the Budget Payment Plan, which is voluntary, you can make regular payments towards a future tax liability. The plan is flexible and you:

- decide the regular weekly or monthly amount you want to pay to HMRC;

- can choose to amend your regular payment amount;

- are free to take a break or suspend payment for a period of up to six months; and

- can cancel the Budget Payment Plan at any time.

The payments you make:

- are in advance; and

- reduce what you have to pay on either the following 31 January or 31 July.

You must still pay the full amount of tax by the due date.

Certificates of tax deposit

You can provide for the payment of a future tax liability by purchasing a Certificate of Tax Deposit. The main features of such certificates are:

- the minimum first deposit is £500;

- subsequent deposits must be at least £250;

- they earn interest from the date of purchase to the normal due date for payment of the tax; and

- the interest is taxable.

Date of receipt

Tax payments are considered to be received by your Accounts Office as follows:

Payment Method	Effective Date of Payment
Received by post (except below)	day of receipt by HMRC
Received by post following a day when the office has been closed for whatever reason (including a weekend)	the day the office was first closed (for payments received on Monday, the effective date will be the previous Saturday)
Electronic Funds Transfer (EFT) – payment by BACS or CHAPS (Clearing House Automated Payment System)	one working day immediately before the date that the value is received. (A working day is defined as a Bank of England working day)
Bank Giro or Girobank	three working days before the date of processing by HMRC

Interest

You will be charged interest if you are late in paying your tax. The rate is Bank base rate plus 2.5%. At the time of going to print, this works out at 3%. It is calculated from the due date until the payment of the tax. Tax relief on the interest is not allowed.

There may be circumstances when the imposition of interest would not be fair to you and can be justifiably contested. HMRC's Code of Practice entitled 'Mistakes by HMRC' points out that an Inspector will waive interest where delays have occurred for more than six months over and above the twenty-eight-day target for dealing with such matters. The booklet goes on to say:

'If there is no good reason for a delay, and we have taken more than six months in total – over and above the twenty-eight-day target we have set ourselves – we will, for amounts unpaid, or not repaid, because of our delay:

- give up interest that arose on unpaid tax during the period of our delay; or

- pay you interest (called 'repayment interest') on money we owed you during the period of our delay; and

- pay any reasonable costs which you have incurred as a direct result of our delay.'

You will be paid interest, which is called repayment supplement and is not taxable, by HMRC on overpayment of any of the following:

- payments on account of Income Tax;

- Income tax and Capital Gains Tax;

- surcharges on late payment of tax;

- any penalties imposed.

The formula for working out the interest rate on repayments is Bank base rate minus 1% but with a minimum rate of 0.5%.

Remission of tax

Arrears of Income Tax or Capital Gains Tax may be waived if they result from HMRC's failure to make proper and timely use of information supplied by:

- the taxpayer about his or her own income, capital gains or personal circumstances;

- an employer, where the information affects an employee's notice of coding; or

- the DWP about a taxpayer's retirement, disability or widow's State Pension.

The concession is normally only given where the taxpayer:

- could reasonably have believed that his or her tax affairs were in order; and

- is notified of the arrears by the end of the tax year following that in which it arose.

Surcharges

Surcharges are levied on late payment of Income Tax, but not payments on account, or Capital Gains Tax as follows:

Tax unpaid by 28 February
(one month after the tax was due)   5% of unpaid tax

Tax unpaid by 31 July
(six months after the tax was due)   Further 5% of tax unpaid

A surcharge notice must be formally served on you by HMRC. You have 30 days in which to appeal against the notice if you think you have a reasonable excuse for late payment of the tax. Your appeal might be successful:

- if there is clear evidence that your cheque was lost in the post; or

- in the event of serious illness.

Examples of circumstances where your appeal will be rejected are:

- cheques wrongly made out; and

- lack of funds other than for exceptional reasons.

Penalties

The main penalties under Self-Assessment are:

Offence	Penalty
You do not submit a paper Tax Return to your Tax Office by 31 October after the end of the tax year	£100
Your do not file online by 31 January after the end of the tax year	£100
Your Return is still outstanding by the following 31 July	Further £100

These penalties will be reduced to the amount of tax owing where this is less than £100.

Where taxpayers have a genuinely good excuse for missing the annual filing deadline for submitting Tax Returns they can appeal against the automatic late filing penalty.

What may be accepted by HMRC as a reasonable excuse for late filing include:

- where the Tax Return was not received by the taxpayer;
- where the Tax Return was lost in the post or delayed because of:
  - fire or flood at the post office where the Tax Return was handled;
  - prolonged industrial action within the post office;
  - an unforeseen event which disrupted the postal services;
- where a taxpayer lost his or her tax records as a result of fire, flood or theft;
- serious illness;
- death of a spouse, domestic partner or close relative.

HMRC will not agree the following as a reasonable excuse for being late:

- Tax Return too difficult;
- pressure of work;
- lack of information; or
- absence of reminders from HMRC.

The other penalties are:

Offence	*Penalty*
Late returns	**Up to £60 per day extra on application to the Commissioners by HMRC**
Returns still outstanding after the anniversary of the previous 31 January	**£200 and a further sum up to the amount of the tax payable**

You do not receive a Tax Return and fail to notify HMRC of chargeability to tax within six months of the end of the tax year	% of the tax payable: (a) None if the failure is not deliberate (b) 30% for a careless oversight (c) 70% for a deliberate but not concealed failure (d) 100% if the failure was both deliberate and concealed
Failure to maintain and keep records	Up to £3,000
Fraudulently or negligently claiming to reduce interim tax payments have been paid	Up to an amount equivalent to the difference between the tax paid and the tax that should have been paid

Generally a penalty determination must be made, or proceedings commence, within six years of the date on which the penalty was incurred. The Rules allow for this period of time to be extended to any later date within three years of the final determination of the tax liability.

The penalty regime for errors on documents and returns:

- depends on why you made the error; and

- how serious was the reason.

HMRC use penalties to stop individuals who do not take care with their tax affairs from gaining an unfair advantage.

If you take reasonable care to get it right, HMRC will not charge a penalty where an error occurs. Some of the ways you can demonstrate you took reasonable care are:

- keeping accurate records and updating them regularly so you can make sure your Tax Returns are correct;

- saving your records should you need them at a later date;

- checking what the correct position is when you do not understand something or, alternatively, seeking advice from HMRC or a competent tax advisor;

- telling HMRC as soon as possible about any error you discover after sending in a tax return or other document.

If you do not take reasonable care HMRC can penalise any errors and these will be higher if the errors are deliberate.

What if you have to pay a penalty? HMRC will:

- contact you to discuss your tax;

- discuss the reason for the error – the more serious the reason, the higher the tax penalty can be;

- reduce the penalty if you help them work out the correct tax due;

- explain why they are issuing a penalty and will send you a penalty notice.

HMRC can substantially reduce any penalty due if you:

- tell HMRC about any errors without being prompted by them;

- help HMRC work out if any extra tax is due;

- allow them to check your figures.

The penalty is a percentage of the extra tax due and depends on why you made the error as follows:

Reason	Rate of Penalty	
	Maximum	**Minimum**
Reasonable Care	No penalty	
Carelessness	30%	0%
Deliberate	70%	20%
Deliberate and concealed	100%	30%

You will have to pay the tax and any interest due, as well as the penalty.

If you incur a penalty because you failed to take reasonable care with your tax affairs, HMRC can suspend it for up to two years. In that time you need to get your systems right. If then you meet all the conditions laid down by HMRC the penalty will be cancelled.

You always have the right of appeal where you think that a penalty is unfair.

16   ELECTIONS AND CLAIMS – TIME LIMITS

You will already have gathered that certain options available to you as a taxpayer are dependent on you submitting an election or making a claim to HMRC. As these will usually involve a saving in tax it is important to appreciate that you often need to act within prescribed time limits. This chapter brings together those elections and claims that are most likely to be of relevance to you. It also sets out the time limit for submission to HMRC. It is by no means exhaustive.

Chapter 2 – Tax Rates and Allowances

Election/Claim	Time Limit
The various elections for the transfer of the married couple's and blind person's allowances	Generally before the start of the tax year for which it is to have effect
Claim to the personal allowances detailed in the chapter	No later than four years after 31 January next following the end of the tax year
Transfer of excess allowances between husband and wife	No later than four years after 31 January next following the end of the tax year

Chapter 3 – Tax Credits

Election/Claim	Time Limit
Claims for Tax Credits	Claims will only be backdated by a maximum of three months
Annual renewal	By 31 July following the end of a tax year

Chapter 4 – Interest Payments and other Outgoings

Election/Claim	Time Limit
Election to treat charity donations under Gift Aid as made in the previous tax year	On or before when you deliver your tax return for the previous year but not later than 31 January after the tax year

Chapter 6 – Value Added Tax

Election/Claim	Time Limit
Application for Registration	No later than 30 days from the end of the month after the one when turnover exceeds the registration limit
Claim for Bad Debt Relief	When a debt remains unpaid for more than six months

Chapter 7 – Working for Yourself

Election/Claim	Time Limit
Relief for post-cessation expenses	No later than one year after 31 January next following the tax year in which the payments are made
Creating a separate pool to work out the capital allowances on an asset with a short life expectancy	No later than one year after 31 January next following the tax year in which the period of account ended in which the expenditure is incurred
Relief for the loss sustained in the the tax year against other income of the same year or the preceding year	Within one year after 31 January next following the tax year in which the loss arose
Relief for a trading loss against the profits arising from the same trade in subsequent periods	Within four years after 31 January next following the tax year in which the loss was sustained
Relief for the loss in the first four years of assessment of a new business to be given against the income of the three preceding years of assessment	No later than one year after 31 January next following the tax year in which the loss occurred
Relief for trading losses to be offset against capital gains	No later than one year after 31 January next following the tax year

Relief for the loss in the last 12 months of trading to be given against the profits of the same trade which were assessed in the three tax years prior to the year in which the trade was discontinued	Within four years after 31 January next following the tax year in which the trade ceased

Chapter 10 – Savings and Investment Income

Election/Claim	*Time Limit*
An election to opt out of Rent-a-Room relief for a particular tax year, or withdrawal of an election	Within one year after 31 January next following the tax year
An election for the alternative basis of Rent-a-Room relief, or revocation of an election	Within one year after 31 January next following the tax year
Claim for Income Tax relief under the Enterprise Investment Scheme	Within four years after 31 January next following that in which the shares were issued
Declaration by a married couple or civil partners that their beneficial interest in joint property and the income arising from it are unequal	The date of the declaration which must be sent to HMRC within 60 days

Chapter 13 – Capital Gains

Election/Claim	*Time Limit*
Claim to the capital loss where the value of an asset becomes negligible	The loss arises on the date of claim although, in practice, a two-year period is allowed from the end of the tax year in which the asset became of negligible value
Claim for the loss on shares that were originally subscribed for in an unquoted trading company to be set against income in the year of loss, or the preceding year	No later than one year after 31 January next following the tax year in which the loss was made

Claim to Entrepreneurs' Relief	No later than one year after 31 January next following the tax year in which the disposal took place
An election to determine which of your homes is to be regarded as your principal residence for Capital Gains Tax purposes	Two years from the date when two or more properties are eligible

17   INHERITANCE TAX

Inheritance Tax is payable on:

- any chargeable transfers you make during your lifetime; and
- the value of your estate on death.

There are a number of exemptions and reliefs which, if optimised, can reduce the amount of tax payable, perhaps significantly.

As with all types of direct taxation, husband and wife are treated as separate individuals.

Inheritance Tax is administered by the Inheritance Tax Offices of HMRC in England and Scotland to whom all Returns, Accounts and payments of tax should be submitted.

Some of the aspects of the tax, particularly those relating to agricultural and business property as well as transfers into Trusts, are complex. Therefore, what follows is a resumé of the main areas of the tax which are likely to be of most relevance and interest to you.

Potentially exempt transfers

Perhaps the most significant feature of Inheritance Tax is that of a potentially exempt transfer (PET). This is:

- an outright gift to an individual;
- a gift into settlement for the benefit of a disabled person;
- certain other transfers into trust.

No tax is payable providing the donor survives for at least seven years from the date of making the gift.

Chargeable lifetime gifts

Any gift or transfer which is not potentially exempt is liable to Inheritance

Tax when it is made. Typically, many gifts into settlement are chargeable transfers. In working out the Inheritance Tax at the date of gift:

- it is only the excess, if any, over the nil rate band on which tax is payable;

- the rate of tax is one-half of the rate applicable on death at the time.

Gifts with reservation and pre-owned assets

If you make a gift but carry on enjoying some benefit from the property or asset, it is still likely to be regarded as yours until either:

- the date when you stop enjoying any benefit from the gift; or

- your death.

This is what is known as a 'gift with reservation'. For example, you give your home to your children but continue living there, rent free. Your home will still be in your estate.

You also have to pay income tax each year on the value of any assets that you continue to use or enjoy after you have given them away.

Exemptions

The main exemptions for individuals are:

- transfers, without limit, between husband and wife – both during lifetime and on death;

- similarly between civil partners;

- gifts up to £3,000 in any one tax year. Any part of the exemption that is unused can be carried forward, but to the following year only;

Nancy Young gave her brother £1,800 in August 2009. A year later, she wanted to make a more substantial gift, but this time to her sister. She was able to give away £4,200 in September 2010, within her annual exemption limits for 2009/10 and 2010/11 as follows:

2009/10	£
Annual exemption limit	3,000
Less: Gift to brother	1,800
Carried forward to next year	1,200
2010/11	
Annual exemption limit	3,000
Gift to sister	£4,200

If Nancy had given her brother £3,000 in August 2009, she would have been limited to gifting the same amount to her sister in 2010/11.

- gifts to any number of persons, but only up to £250 per person in each tax year. Where the total amount given to any one individual exceeds the amount of £250 then no part of the gift comes within the exemption;

- marriage gifts. The amount you can give away in consideration of marriage or civil partnership depends on your relationship to the bride, groom or civil partner, as follows:

	£
By either parent	**5,000**
By a grandparent or great grandparent	**2,500**
By any other person	**1,000**

- regular gifts out of income which form part of your normal expenditure;

Glyn Fielding, who lives alone, has an annual after-tax income of around £30,000. He has a modest lifestyle. He spends about £20,000 a year on his home, food, recreation, holidays and other living expenses.

His brother, Luke, who is married, is not so fortunate. Glyn could make regular gifts to his brother out of his annual surplus income of £10,000, free of Inheritance Tax.

* lifetime gifts and bequests on death to charities and 'qualifying' political parties, without limit.

Business property

Transfers in lifetime or on death, subject to certain conditions, of eligible business assets and interests in businesses qualify for relief from Inheritance Tax. There are two rates:

100% for:

* unincorporated businesses;
* all holdings of unquoted shares in qualifying companies;
* unquoted shares, including those traded on the AIM market.

50% for:

* shares giving control of a quoted company;
* land, buildings, machinery or plant used in a partnership or controlled company where the transferor is a partner or controlling shareholder.

Agricultural property

The reliefs applying to agricultural land and buildings are similar to those for business property. Subject to certain minimum ownership and use conditions, the two rates are again:

100% for:

* land and buildings where the transferor has vacant possession, or the right to obtain it, within twelve months;
* agricultural property let for periods exceeding twelve months where letting commenced on or after 1 September 1995;

50% for:

* other qualifying property.

Rates of tax payable

From 6 April 2010, Inheritance Tax is payable on:

• all transfers or gifts within three years of death; and

• on death.

This is determined by the following table:

Cumulative chargeable transfers	Rate
£	%
0–325,000	0
Over 325,000	40

The tax due on each chargeable gift or the value of your estate on death is dependent upon the cumulative value of all other chargeable transfers in the previous seven years.

Taper relief

A method of tapering relief applies where a donor dies within seven years of making a transfer. It is not the gift, but the amount of tax, that is reduced. The Inheritance Tax is worked out at the rate prevailing as at the date of death and then reduced in accordance with the following table:

Number of years between gift and death	% of IHT payable
Not more than 3	100
Between 3 and 4	80
Between 4 and 5	60
Between 5 and 6	40
Between 6 and 7	20

Gavin Wood, a bachelor, made his nephew, Rhys, a cash gift of £350,000 in May 2005. Gavin died in November 2010, leaving an estate of £400,000.

As Gavin did not survive for seven years, Rhys has to pay tax of £3,040 on his gift, calculated as follows:

	£
Cash gift	350,000
Less: Gavin's annual exemption limits for 2004/05 and 2005/06	6,000
	344,000
Less: Nil Rate Band at the date of Gavin's death	325,000
Tax payable on	£19,000
Inheritance Tax thereon @ 40%	7,600
Less: Taper Relief (60% for surviving five years)	4,560
Tax payable	£3,040

It follows that there is no benefit of tapering relief where a PET, or the cumulative total of a number of PETs combined with any chargeable lifetime transfers, is within the limit of the nil rate band as at the date of death.

Transferable nil rate band

Any part of the nil rate band not used on the first death of a married couple or civil partners is not lost. It is available to all survivors of a marriage or civil partnership.

It does not matter when the first spouse of a marriage died; it can have occurred at any time. However, for civil partnerships, the first death must be later than 4 December 2005 when the Civil Partnership Act came into effect.

Any amount of the unused nil rate band can only be transferred from one spouse to the surviving spouse when their relationship is ended by the death of one of them. In cases of divorce, and where one party to the broken marriage subsequently dies, the relief will not be available.

On the death of the survivor:

- the percentage limit of the nil rate band applying on the death of the first spouse or civil partner which was unused is applied to the nil rate band when the survivor dies; and

- the resulting amount is added to the survivor's own nil rate band.

> Melvin Churchill died on 4 January 2005, leaving his estate of £200,000 to his wife, Eileen. She passed away on 10 December 2010, with an estate worth £600,000 divided between their four children.
>
> When Melvin died, no part of the nil rate band at the time of £263,000 was used. Therefore, the nil rate band on Eileen's death is doubled to £650,000 and there is no Inheritance Tax to pay on her death.

> Janice Timms died on 21 July 1996. Her estate amounted to £400,000. In her will she left legacies of £60,000 to each of her two children and the balance of her wealth to her husband, Colin. He passed away on 9 February 2011, worth £620,000 spread equally between the two children.
>
> When Janice died the nil rate band was £200,000 of which 60% (£120,000) was used against the legacies to her two children, leaving 40% to transfer to Colin on his death earlier this year. Colin's nil rate band of £325,000 is increased by 40% to £455,000, leaving Inheritance Tax at 40% payable on £165,000.

Death

When someone dies, their assets pass into their estate to be administered by their personal representatives. Their main duties and responsibilities are to:

- gather in the assets of the deceased;

- settle their debts;

- pay out any legacies; and then

- distribute their remaining assets to the residuary beneficiaries.

It is also necessary to complete an Inheritance Tax Return and submit the form together with an application for a grant of:

- Probate where there is a will; or

- Administration where there is no will.

The Return must:

- be lodged within twelve months of the date of death;

- include information about previous transfers and gifts in order that the amount of Inheritance Tax payable can be calculated.

In order to help your executors when the time comes, you are well advised to maintain:

- up-to-date details of all your assets and where the supporting certificates and documents are stored;

- complete records of your lifetime gifts.

Conrad Huxtable, a widower, died on 14 May 2010, leaving his entire estate to his son. He did not make any gifts in the seven years leading up to his death. His assets and unpaid bills at the time were:

Assets		Value
	£	£
Home	360,000	
Household effects	4,000	
Car	3,000	
Building society account	20,000	
National Savings	8,000	
Individual Savings Accounts	13,000	
Bank current account	1,500	
Outstanding State Pension	540	
Cash	60	
		410,100
Less: Allowable Deductions		
Funeral expenses	1,410	
Income tax	620	
Household bills	440	
Car repair	230	
		2,700
Net Value of Estate		£407,400
Inheritance Tax payable		
On first £325,000		Nil
On next £82,400 at 40%		32,960
		£32,960

The tax is payable out of Conrad Huxtable's estate by the executors of his will.

Sales at a loss

Relief from Inheritance Tax is due on certain assets sold within specified time limits after death for less than their values at the date of death:

- for quoted securities the period is one year;

- in the case of land and buildings, the time limit extends to four years.

The relief is available to the 'appropriate person', namely the person who pays the tax. All sales by that person in the respective periods must be aggregated. As a result, losses can be restricted or eliminated by profits so that the relief may be reduced or even lost. When this type of relief is claimed, the sale proceeds, before selling expenses, are substituted for the valuation at death. The Inheritance Tax liability is then reworked.

Payment of tax

Primarily liable for the payment of Inheritance Tax are:

- the transferor in respect of chargeable lifetime gifts;

- the personal representatives on death.

Personal representatives can draw on funds held in a deceased's bank and building society accounts solely for the purpose of paying any Inheritance Tax that is due before the Grant of Probate can be issued. The payment dates for Inheritance Tax are:

Type of Charge	Due date for payment
Chargeable Lifetime Gifts	six months after the end of the month in which the gift was made
PETs which become taxable on death,and the charge on death itself	six months after the end of the month in which death occurred

There is an option to pay the tax due on some types of asset by ten equal annual instalments. For lifetime transfers which are, or become, chargeable, this instalment option is only available if the tax is borne by the transferee. The first amount is, however, payable on the normal due date.

The assets concerned are:

- land and buildings;
- controlling shareholdings;
- unquoted shares, subject to certain conditions; and
- businesses.

Where the relevant asset is disposed of during the instalment paying period, all the outstanding instalments of Inheritance Tax become immediately payable.

Interest and penalties

Interest is chargeable on Inheritance Tax liabilities from the due date until the date of payment. At the time of going to print, the rate of interest is 3%. Any repayment of tax or interest thereon carries interest presently at the much lower rate of 0.5% for the period from the date it was paid until it is refunded.

Where the instalment option is in effect, no interest is charged on the outstanding instalments of Inheritance Tax, except on:

- land and buildings which do not qualify for either business or agricultural property reliefs; and
- shares and securities in investment companies.

As with your Tax Return, there are penalties for late or incorrect Returns, delays, negligence or fraud as well as the late payment of Inheritance Tax.

Intestacy

If you die without having made a will, your estate will be distributed under the Intestate Estate Rules. There are two tables; one for an unmarried individual and the other for a person with a surviving spouse.

The existing intestacy rules for individuals who die domiciled in England and Wales are as follows:

Unmarried individual

Survived by

Children or grandchildren	The total estate is shared in
Parents	the following order of
Brothers and sisters	priority, to the exclusion of
Half-brothers and half-sisters	all others
Grandparents	
Uncles and aunts	
The Crown	

Married individual

Particular Circumstances		Division
(1)	Estate amounts to less than £250,000	All to spouse
(2)	Estate exceeds £250,000 and there are children	Spouse is entitled to first £250,000 and a life interest in half the remainder. The balance is shared between the children
(3)	Estate is worth less than £450,000 and there are no children	All to spouse
(4)	Estate comes to more than £450,000, the couple have no children but parents are still alive	Spouse receives first £450,000 and half the remainder absolutely. The parents divide the rest
(5)	As in (4) above, parents are dead, but there are brothers and sisters	As in (4) above, but the balance is shared between the brothers and sisters instead of the parents
(6)	The only survivor is the spouse	All to spouse

The spouse must survive the intestate individual by 28 days to become entitled under the intestacy rules.

Civil partners, and the children of a civil partnership, benefit under the intestacy rules in the same way as spouses and the children of a marriage.

In Scotland the intestacy rules have no application to estates of individuals who die domiciled there. Furthermore, a surviving spouse and/or children are entitled to fixed proportions of the moveable estate of the deceased individual. This rule applies whether the deceased died intestate or had made a will.

Legacies

If you are fortunate enough to receive a legacy from a member of your family or a friend:

- any Inheritance Tax on a legacy will be accounted for by the executors before you receive it;
- you do not have to pay either Income Tax or Capital Gains Tax on a legacy;
- it does not need to be reported on your annual Tax Return.

18 TAX-SAVING POINTERS

Throughout all the stages of life, from the time we are born until the day we die, decisions need to be taken on our tax and financial affairs. During our years of minority these are dealt with by our parents. When we reach adulthood at age 18, which is about the time we leave school and head for university, we become responsible for everything in life including tax and dealing with HMRC. After university comes a life of work, most likely for someone else, but maybe for ourselves in self-employment. In this period of the cycle of life we:

- are likely to get married or enter a civil partnership;

- may buy our own home;

- will want to save through a pension and make investments to provide for the day when we retire.

Our years in retirement:

- are most likely to be those when we will need to maximise our income from pensions and savings; and

- are probably those when we will concentrate on doing what we can to minimise the amount of our estates that goes on death duties – Inheritance Tax.

At every stage it is important to make well-informed decisions to ensure that we follow the best strategies for achieving our goals. When it comes to tax:

- we may need to adjust our finances to take account of future increases or reductions in the various taxes;

- we should not consider saving tax without having due regard to other criteria; and

- we should always be ready to respond to any shift in tax policy following a change in Government.

I like to think that somewhere in the following sections you will find pointers to help you save on tax.

Childhood and teenage years

- Do not miss out on collecting your Child Benefit. It does not depend on income and is tax-free.

- If you are on a low or modest income you should be able to claim the Child Tax Credit. Do not delay in making your claim since it can only be backdated for a maximum of three months.

- Children's Bonus Bonds, issued by National Savings and Investments, are totally tax-free and particularly suitable for investing gifts from parents.

- Like any other taxpayer children and teenagers are allowed income of £6,475 for 2010/11 before paying tax.

Tax compliance

- First and foremost, keep proper and orderly records. This will make it easier for you to complete your Tax Return fully and accurately. Furthermore, if your tax office decides to enquire into your Tax Return the records you have maintained will enable you to demonstrate that the Return is both accurate and complete.

- Also remember to keep your records for the right length of time. This is much longer if you are self-employed or letting property.

- Make sure you fill in your Tax Return properly by only writing in the spaces provided using blue or black ink and using numbers, without pence, when asked for amounts.

- If the amount of any of your sources of income is substantially different compared to the previous year, use the additional information box on page TR6 to explain the reason for the change.

- If you have paid too much tax complete your Tax Return as soon as after the end of the tax year to get your money back. HMRC will refund the overpayment direct to your bank or building society account. This is the safest and quickest method. Always fill in the boxes 4–14 on page TR5 as appropriate.

- Remember that you can amend your self-assessment at any time in the 12 month period after the latest 31 January filing deadline.

- Do not forget to sign the Return. This is one of the most common mistakes that HMRC have found when processing Tax Returns.

- Other errors include failing to complete the self-employed pages and a separate supplementary page for each individual employment.

- Do not overlook the new reduced time limit for making some elections and claims.

- Make your charitable donations under the Gift Aid Scheme. The tax you deduct and retain at the basic rate will then be refunded by HMRC to your chosen charities.

- Furthermore, if you pay tax above the basic rate, you will also gain as you can deduct the grossed up equivalent of your donations under Gift Aid in working out how much tax you pay at either the 40% or 50% rates.

- But if you give assets, instead of cash, to a charity you can save on both Income Tax and Capital Gains Tax

- Remember the key dates in the self-assessment calendar which are summarised in Appendix 8 at the end of the book.

- Of particular importance are the two dates for sending back your Tax Return each year. These are 31 October (for paper filing) and 31 January (for online filing) after the end of the tax year. You must send your Return back by 31 October if you want HMRC to work out your tax bill.

- The 31 October deadline for paper filing also applies if you pay tax under PAYE, and want any tax underpayment of less than £2,000 collected by an adjustment to your PAYE code in the following year. For online filing this is extended by two months to 30 December. There is no interest or other charge for spreading out the underpayment over income received in the following year.

- Do not forget that both send-back dates of 31 October (for paper) and 31 January (online) are critical. You must stick to them otherwise you will be charged a fixed £100 penalty for filing a late Return.

- Always pay your tax on time. If you are late in making payment then not only will you be charged interest but you will also run the risk of incurring a surcharge.

- If your income for 2011/12 from all sources is likely to be less than 2010/11, apply to HMRC for reduced payments on account.

In employment

- Contributions made by your employer to a company pension scheme in which you participate or into your own personal pension plan are not taxable on you.

- Perhaps your net income is somewhere between £100,000 and £112,950 (£114,950 for 2011/12). The marginal tax rate on income in this band is 60% or $37^{1}/_{2}$% on net dividends. In such circumstances, the payment of allowable pension contributions and Gift Aid donations is very tax efficient.

- There are not many employment related expenses on which you can claim tax relief but you are allowed tax relief on subscriptions to a professional body and on the cost of clothing and upkeep of tools in most classes of industry as set out in Appendix 2.

- Find out whether your employer operates one of the various share, profit-sharing and share option, schemes all of which have different investment limits and levels of tax relief. Membership of whatever scheme is on offer may be an attractive long-term investment with built-in tax advantages.

- For many employees the company car continues to be an important part of the remuneration package. The system of taxing company cars is geared towards encouraging the cleaner use of cars by linking the tax charge to the exhaust emission of the car. When the time comes for you to change your company car it will pay you to look into the carbon dioxide emission of the proposed replacement car. You will save tax on your company car benefit by opting for a car with a lower approved CO_2 emission figure.

- The cost of petrol or diesel for your private mileage paid by your employer is a taxable benefit worked out on the CO_2 emission figure for your car. You will often be better off paying for your own fuel for non-business travel.

- Sometimes it is better to own your car and charge your employer for the cost of all your business mileage but you must keep a proper and detailed log of all business and private mileage.

- If your employer pays you a mileage allowance for using your car, motorcycle or bicycle for business you can claim tax relief on any difference between the amount you receive and the statutory rate.

- Remember that there is no tax charge on parking spaces provided at, or near, your workplace.

- Around January/February each year look out for your new PAYE Coding Notice for the following tax year. Check it carefully to make sure you have been given the right allowances and that any deductions for unpaid tax or benefits-in-kind are correct. Get in touch with your Tax Office if anything is not right.

- Check that you have not overpaid on National Insurance contributions. This is likely to happen if you have more than one job, or you are in work and self-employed at the same time. Excess contributions can be reclaimed from HMRC after the end of the tax year.

Working for yourself – tax

- Do not forget to advise HMRC as soon as you begin self-employment.

- Then think about your accounting date. 31 March is an obvious and convenient choice as the date coincides with the end of the tax year on 5 April. However, it is sometimes preferable to go with a date early on in the tax year, such as 30 April, as it allows you more time to plan for the funding of the tax payable.

- Alternatively, if your business is seasonal in nature, it may be a good idea to pick an annual accounting date to coincide with the slack time of the year and when stocks are low.

- Maintain proper accounting records for your business. Make sure they are accurate and always up-to-date.

- Avoid using estimates for some business expenses. If they are challenged on enquiry by HMRC you will find it difficult to substantiate the claim in your accounts.

- Where you incur mixed expenses – part business with the balance private – be careful over the apportionment calculation and only claim the proper and reasonable business element as an expense for tax purposes.

- Maybe you need to buy some plant or machinery or, perhaps a new car for your business. There are 100% allowances in the first year on:
  — purchases of plant and machinery up to £100,000 by a small business;
  — purchases of new electric vans; and
  — expenditure on low emission or electrically propelled cars.

- It may be tax efficient to incur this expenditure towards the end of the accounting year rather than early on in the following year. You will then benefit from the capital allowances due on the expenditure at an earlier date.

- Where appropriate pay your spouse or partner a fair and justifiable salary for secretarial or other assistance given to you.

- Look into taking your spouse/partner into partnership where he or she helps you in the business and your annual profits are such that the top slice is taxable at the higher 40% or additional 50% rates. Between you it may be possible to make significant savings in your overall annual tax bill.

- Consider all the different options for claiming the tax relief due if your business has made a loss.

- There are special rules for losses incurred by either new businesses or those that have just closed down.

- Make sure you claim your entitlement to the Small Business Rate Relief. This allows small businesses a reduction of up to 50% of their full charge for rates.

- If your business is booming and is extremely profitable you should seriously think about transferring it to a Limited company where you own the shares. You may well be able to reduce your overall tax burden but it is an area where you should seek advice from a tax specialist.

- Alternatively, in the current difficult economic climate, your business may be faced with cash flow problems. Telephone the new HMRC Business Payment Support Service for help in spreading the payment of present and future tax bills.

- Finally, always look to the future and plan for your retirement whether you be contemplating a sale of your business or handing it down to the next generation.

Working for yourself – Value Added Tax

- If your business is not within VAT, plan ahead so you know when to register. Then maintain a regular check on your turnover to make sure you are not exceeding the limit for registration.

- Sometimes it pays to apply for voluntary registration. You may be able to reclaim significant amounts of VAT on purchases for, and expenses of your business. However, it is worth checking on your customers to make sure that they are VAT registered and will be able to recover the VAT charged on your invoices.

- Make sure you submit each VAT Return and pay what is due to HMRC within the stipulated time limit.

- If the annual turnover of your business is under the qualifying amount perhaps the Flat Rate Scheme is for you. It will save you time in dealing with the requirements of normal accounting for VAT.

- Look into the respective merits of the Annual or Cash Accounting Schemes. They have the same turnover limits for you to be able to participate in them.

- Always speak up if things go wrong or if there is something you do not understand. HMRC generally want to help you get things right. Always give the full facts and quote your VAT number.

Income from savings

- Non-taxpayers (such as some pensioners, children or dependent married spouses) should get the special form so they can apply to receive their bank and building society interest without any deduction for tax. This will save them having to claim a tax refund from HMRC.

- Married couples and civil partners should look to see whether they need to transfer their income producing assets between them in order to maximize their entitlement to personal allowances and the basic rate tax band. If, for some reason, this is inappropriate, joint ownership might be an alternative.

- Individuals in the top tax brackets should take a look at those investments available from National Savings and Investments where the return is free of both Income Tax and Capital Gains Tax.

- If you are contemplating the purchase of a property which you are then going to let out as an investment it may well pay you to take out a loan to assist in financing the purchase. You will be able to claim the annual interest on the borrowing as a deduction from the net rental income of the property.

- Properties let out as Furnished Holiday Accommodation qualify for many tax concessions, including income tax relief on losses from running the business.

- Alternatively remortgage your buy to let property releasing funds for other uses and still get tax relief on the interest.

- If you are a landlord don't overlook the one-off allowance of up to £1,500 per property on energy saving insulation available on expenditure up to 5 April 2015. This covers floor, wall, loft and hot-water systems.

- If you can don't miss out on investing the maximum amount each year in an ISA:

  — the annual ISA investment allowance is £10,200;

  — up to £5,100 of that allowance can be saved in cash with one provider;

  — the remainder of the annual allowance can be invested in stocks and shares with either the same or another provider; and

  — you can transfer monies saved in cash ISAs into stocks and shares ISAs.

- You can withdraw up to 5% per annum tax-free each year from a non-qualifying life policy such as a single premium investment bond. This could be a good way to supplement your income, particularly for anyone in the top tax brackets.

- Venture Capital Trusts are tax-efficient vehicles aimed at encouraging investment in unquoted companies in the UK. Bear in mind, therefore, that an investment in a Venture Capital Trust carries a higher degree of risk. The tax benefits for a 'qualifying subscriber' are 30% income tax relief on the amount invested up to £200,000 along with tax-free income and capital gains after five years.

- Investments under the Enterprise Investment Scheme are also high risk with generous tax benefits.

- Non-resident married couples or civil partners with let property in the United Kingdom should think about putting their properties into joint ownership. It might then be possible for both parties to claim their personal allowance in working out the tax payable on their respective shares of the rental income.

- Non-domiciled foreign nationals living in the UK should take professional advice about whether they should be taxed for the year:

  — on the remittance basis and pay the annual charge of £30,000; or

  — on the arising basis.

Capital profits

- Wherever possible try to utilize all your Capital Gains Tax exemption limit each year. Any unused part of the annual limit cannot be carried forward to future years, it is lost.

- By realizing gains just after the end of the tax year will delay payment of the tax for 12 months.

- By splitting sales across the end of a tax year you can make use of your annual exemption limit for two years.

- Husband and wife, as do civil partners, each have their own annual exemption limit. They should consider transferring assets between them, to use up both exemption limits.

- But this does not apply for married couples or civil partners who separate. The opportunity to transfer assets between them free of Capital Gains Tax terminates at the end of the tax year in which separation takes place. The moral here is to separate early on in a tax year to allow sufficient time to divide up valuable assets such as land and shares.

- In working out your gains don't forget to take into account all allowable buying and selling expenses and other costs, such as improvements or alterations to buy-to-lets or a second home.

- Following the changes to Capital Gains Tax from 23 June 2010, make sure you claim your annual exemption limit and any losses in the most tax effective way. By doing so you will be able to maximise the amount of gains taxable at only 18% in 2010/11.

- You can claim losses for any assets which you own that have become worthless. In some cases the loss can be offset against income giving you a bigger tax refund.

- Maybe you have disposed of some assets and are looking at a substantial Capital Gains Tax charge on the profits made? Why not consider reinvesting under the Enterprise Investment Scheme? Only the gain, not the sale proceeds, needs to be reinvested so that you can apply to defer the Capital Gains Tax on the gain.

- Look into structuring the ownership of your business so that not only you, but also other family members may be entitled to the new Entrepreneurs' Relief in working out the Capital Gains Tax payable on the profit on a future sale or disposal of the business.

Your home

- As you do not get tax relief on mortgage interest to buy your own home it might be worthwhile using any spare cash on deposit with a bank or building society to repay some or all of your mortgage.

- If you need more income and do not want to move home, take in a lodger or bed and breakfast guest. Up to £4,250 a year is tax free under Rent-a-Room relief.

- If you have two or more homes, you are allowed to make an election nominating which one you want to be regarded as your principal private residence for Capital Gains Tax purposes where the profit on sale is free of tax. The election must be made within two years from the date when two or more properties are eligible although it can subsequently be varied.

- The last three years of ownership of a property, which at some point in time has been your only or main residence even by election, are always regarded as though they were lived in by you as the main residence.

- Where a property that has been let has also been occupied as a main residence there is an additional reduction in the taxable gain, relating to the let period, up to a maximum of £40,000.

- Husband and wife or civil partners should consider owning a second home jointly. This could help reduce the Capital Gains Tax payable on a future sale as they may both be able to take advantage of their respective annual exemption limits in working out the tax payable on a profit on sale.

- If your job takes you away from home for up to four years, your period of absence will still count as if you were in occupation of your main residence. The same applies when you work full-time overseas but for an unlimited period.

- It is not uncommon for unmarried couples to each own a home. They may each be able to nominate a main residence for the purposes of Capital Gains Tax.

Retirement

- When in work try to start saving through a pension as soon as you can. You get tax relief on the contributions which, in turn, are invested in a tax-free fund. You can take up to 25% of your fund tax free.

- As you get near to retirement age for State Pension purposes it is a good idea to get a forecast of what pension you will receive from the DWP. This will also show what additional pension you may be able to purchase by the payment of Class 3 (Voluntary) contributions.

- Maybe it is a good idea to delay taking your State Pension. By the time you receive the lump sum for the deferred pension you might be in a lower tax bracket.

- There are rules allowing elderly couples to transfer the married couples allowance between them. This can sometimes save on tax.

- The income limit for the married couples allowance is by reference to the husband's income or the spouse/civil partner with the higher income as the case may be. These rules apply even if entitlement to this allowance arises because of the others age.

- Elderly couples, in particular, need to give great care and attention to their respective incomes. They should make sure that their investments and savings are arranged such that they do not lose out on the higher personal age allowances and the married couples allowance only for pensioners in the over-74 age bracket. They should be mindful of the annual income limit above which allowances are restricted. Those couples on modest incomes may be better off tax-wise transferring capital between themselves.

- Alternatively it may pay them to shift some of their savings income into tax-free investments such as National Savings or ISAs. In either case, by doing so, they may avoid losing some of their age related allowances.

- Pensioners with low incomes can 'top-up' their income by claiming the Pension Credit.

- Grandparents, or other relatives such as uncles and aunts, can tax-efficiently fund for school fees and other expenses of educating or maintaining grandchildren, nieces or nephews. This might be best done via a Trust, but first of all do take professional advice. The income paid out by the Trustees is the children's income for tax purposes. They should be able to reclaim all or part of the tax suffered by the Trustees on the income distribution by offsetting it against their personal allowance.

Estate planning

- First and foremost, make a Will and keep it up-to-date. Otherwise your Estate will devolve under the intestacy laws and maybe not in a way that you want.

- Always bear in mind that gifts and transfers, during lifetime and on death, between husbands/wives and civil partners are exempt from Inheritance Tax.

- Whenever you can afford to do so, make use of the various exemptions detailed in Chapter 17. By doing so throughout your life you may save on the payment of a significant amount of Inheritance Tax.

- The 'normal expenditure out of income' exemption is ideal for dealing with the payment of regular premiums on life policies written in Trust for future generations. As the policy proceeds pass to them free of tax this is, in effect, a substitute for the payment of an Inheritance Tax liability on death which cannot otherwise be avoided.

- Think about rearranging some of your investments so that you can take advantage of the agricultural or business property reliefs. Companies whose shares are quoted on AIM and which are trading companies count as unquoted for business property relief purposes.

- Gifts and legacies to charities are exempt from Inheritance Tax. But there are also attractive Income Tax and Capital Gains Tax benefits for the donor on lifetime gifts of cash, shares or property to a charity.

- Non-exempt gifts or transfers should be made as early as possible to increase your chances of surviving the seven-year period. Make immediately chargeable gifts – for example transfers into settlement – before those that are potentially exempt.

- Give assets that do not qualify for relief before those that do.

- If possible give assets with low values so that they appreciate in the hands of the recipient and outside of your Estate.

- Consider restricting the chargeable legacies for the next generations to an amount equivalent to the nil rate band for Inheritance Tax, leaving the remainder of your Estate to your spouse or civil partner. He or she can then make gifts and hopefully live for a further seven years.

- In the two years after death, consider the use of a Deed of Variation in order to utilise any available exemptions that would otherwise be lost.

And finally

- Remember that tax reliefs and rates can change with little or no warning, particularly on a change in Government. So always be ready to react to any changes in legislation.

19 APPENDICES

1 HMRC (Revenue) Explanatory Booklets and Helpsheets

Booklets

No.	Title
IR 10	Paying the Right Tax on your Earnings and Pension
IR 111	Bank and Building Society Interest: Are you paying tax when you don't need to?
IR 115	Paying for Childcare – Getting Help from you Employer
IR 121	Approaching retirement. A Guide to Tax and National Insurance Contributions
IR 160	HMRC Enquiries under Self-Assessment
IR 177	Share Incentive Plans and Your Entitlement to Benefits
480	Expenses and Benefits: A Tax Guide
ES/FS 1	Employed or Self-Employed for Tax and National Insurance Contributions
HMRC 1	HMRC decisions – What to do if you disagree
HMRC 6	Residence, Domicile and the Remittance Basis
WTC 1	Child Tax Credit and Working Tax Credit: An Introduction
WTC 2	Child Tax Credit and Working Tax Credit: A Guide

Helpsheets

General

HS310	War Widow's and Dependant's Pensions
HS320	Gains on UK Life Assurance policies
HS341	Enterprise Investment Scheme – Income Tax Relief
HS342	Charitable Giving
HS343	Accrued Income Scheme

Employment

HS201	Vouchers, credit cards and tickets
HS202	Living accommodation
HS203	Car Benefits and Car Fuel Benefits
HS207	Non-Taxable Payments or Benefits for Employees
HS208	Payslips and Coding Notices

HS210   Assets provided for private use
HS211   Employment – Residence and Domicile issues

Self-Employment
HS220   More than one business
HS222   How to calculate your taxable profits
HS227   Losses
HS229   Information from your accounts

2   Flat-Rate Allowances for Special Clothing and the Upkeep of Tools – 2010/11

(1)	*Fixed rate for all occupations*	£
	Agricultural	100
	Clothing	60
	Forestry	100
	Quarrying	100
	Brass and copper	120
	Precious metals	100
	Food	60
	Glass	80
	Railways (non-crafts people)	100
	Uniformed prison officers	80
	Uniformed bank and building society employees	60
	Uniformed police officers up to and including Chief Inspector	140
	Uniformed fire fighters and fire officers	80

(2)	*Variable rate depending on category of occupation*	£
	Seamen	140/165
	Iron mining	100/120
	Iron and steel	60/80/140
	Aluminium	60/80/120/140
	Engineering	60/80/120/140
	Shipyards	60/80/100/140
	Vehicles	60/80/140
	Particular engineering	60/80/120/140
	Constructional engineering	60/80/100/140
	Electrical and electricity supply	60/120
	Textiles and textile printing	80/120
	Leather	60/80
	Printing	60/100/140
	Building materials	60/80/120
	Wood and furniture	60/100/120/140

Building	60/80/120/140
Heating	100/120
Public service	60/80
Healthcare	60/100/140

Note The allowances are only available to manual workers who have to bear the cost of upkeep of tools and special clothing. Other employees, such as office staff, cannot claim them.

3 HMRC (VAT) Notices and Leaflets

No.	Title
700	The VAT Guide
700/1	Should I be Registered for VAT?
700/11	Cancelling your Registration
700/12	Filling in your VAT Return
700/15	The Ins and Outs of VAT
700/18	Relief from VAT on Bad Debts
700/21	Keeping Records and Accounts
700/41	Late Registration Penalty
700/42	Misdeclaration Penalty and Repeated Misdeclaration Penalty
700/43	Default Interest
700/45	How to Correct VAT Errors and make Adjustments or Claims
700/50	Default Surcharge
700/58	Treatment of VAT repayment returns and VAT repayment supplement
700/60	Payments on account
727	Retail Schemes
731	Cash Accounting
732	Annual Accounting
733	Flat Rate Scheme for Small Businesses
930	What if I don't pay?
989	Visits by Customs Officers
999	Catalogue of Publications

4   Rates of National Insurance Contributions for 2010/11

CLASS 1 Contributions for Employees

Contributions levied on all weekly earnings above £110.00 but which do not exceed £844.00:

Standard Rate: 11%

Contracted Out: 9.4%

Earnings Threshold	Weekly	£110.00
	Monthly:	£477.00
	Annual:	£5,715.00
Upper Earnings Limit	Weekly:	£844.00
	Monthly:	£3,657.00
	Annual:	£43,875.00

Contributions levied on all weekly earnings in excess of £844.00: 1%

Reduced Rate for Married Women and Widows with a Valid Election Certificate: 4.85%

Rates for Men and Women over State Pensionable Age: Nil

CLASS 2 Contributions for the Self-Employed

Weekly flat rate: £2.40

Small earnings exception: £5,075.00

CLASS 3 Voluntary Contributions

Weekly rate: £12.05

CLASS 4 Contributions for the Self-Employed

On profits between £5,715 and £43,875: 8%

On profits in excess of £43,875: 1%

5 National Insurance Explanatory Leaflets

No.	Title
No.	*Title*
CA02	National Insurance Contributions for self employed people with small earnings
CA07	Unpaid and Late-Paid Contributions
CA08	Voluntary National Insurance Contributions
CA09	National Insurance Contributions for Widows or Widowers
CA10	National Insurance Contributions for Divorcees
CA12	Training for Further Employment and Your National Insurance Record
CA13	National Insurance Contributions for Married Women with Reduced Elections
CA12	National Insurance Contributions for Self-Employed People: Class 2 and Class 4

6 Social Security Benefits

Taxable

Incapacity Benefit after the first 28 weeks (1) (2)
Employment and Support Allowance (contribution-based) (3)
Industrial Death Benefit Pensions
Invalidity Allowance Paid with State Pension
Jobseeker's Allowance
State Retirement Pension (1)
Carer's Allowance (1)
Statutory Adoption Pay
Statutory Maternity and Paternity Pay
Statutory Sick Pay
Widows and Widowers Bereavement Benefits

Non-taxable

Incapacity Benefit for the first 28 weeks (2)
Employment and Support Allowance (income-related) (3)
Income Support
Maternity Allowance
Child Benefit
Child Tax Credit
Child's Special Allowance
Guardian's Allowance
Christmas Bonus for Pensioners
Industrial Injury Benefits
War Disablement Benefits

Disability Living Allowance
Severe Disablement Allowance
Bereavement Payment (Lump Sum)
Earnings Top-Up
Housing Benefit
Jobfinder's Grant
War Pensions
Social Fund Payments
Attendance Allowance
Council Tax Benefit
Redundancy Payment
Vaccine Damage (Lump Sum)
Television Licence Payment
Cold Weather and Winter Fuel Payments
Pension Credit
Working Tax Credit

Note (1) Child dependency additions to these benefits are not taxable.

(2) Existing claimants on 27 October 2008.

(3) Replaced Incapacity Benefit for new claimants from 27 October 2008.

7 Rates of Main Social Security Benefits for 2010/11

Weekly Rate from 12.04.2010 Onwards

£

Taxable

Retirement pensions

Single person	97.65
Married couples: both contributors – each	97.65
wife not contributor – addition	58.50
Age addition (over 80) – each	0.25

Bereavement benefits

Bereavement allowance / widow's pension – maximum	97.65
Widowed parent's allowance	97.65

Jobseeker's allowance

Age 18 to 24	51.85
Age 25 or over	65.45
Couple both 18 or over	102.75

Incapacity benefit

Long-term	91.40
Increase for age: higher rate	15.00
lower rate	5.85
Short-term (under pension age): lower rate	68.95
higher rate	81.60
(over pension age): lower rate	87.75
higher rate	91.40

Statutory sick pay

Standard rate (weekly earnings threshold £97)	79.15

Statutory maternity, paternity and adoption pay

Rate (weekly earnings threshold £97)	124.08

Non-taxable

Maternity allowance

Standard rate	124.08

Child benefit

Only or eldest child (couple or lone parent)	20.30
Each other child	13.40

Attendance allowance

Higher rate	71.40
Lower rate	47.80

8   Main Dates of the Self-Assessment Calendar 6 April 2011 – 5 April 2012

Date	What happens	Who is affected
6 April 2011	2010/11 Tax Returns sent out by HMRC.	Taxpayers who need to fill in an annual Tax Return.
31 July 2011	Second payment on account due for 2010/11.	Those taxpayers who make regular half-yearly payments on account.
	Second £100 penalty levied for failing to submit a 2009/10 Tax Return.	Taxpayers who have not yet completed and sent back their 2009/10 Tax Returns.
	Further automatic 5% surcharge on tax still outstanding for 2009/10.	Late payers of tax still due for 2009/10.
31 October 2011	Filing deadline for completing and returning 2010/11 paper Tax Returns.	Taxpayers who want HMRC to: • calculate their tax for 2010/11; • collect tax owing for 2010/11 of less than £2,000 through their code number in 2012/13.
31 January 2012	Filing deadline for 2010/11 online Tax Returns.	Taxpayers sent a 2010/11 Tax Return.
	Payment date for the balance of tax due for 2010/11 and the first payment on account for 2011/12.	Taxpayers who need to settle either of these liabilities.
1 February 2012	First penalty of £100 charged for the late filing of a 2010/11 Tax Return.	Taxpayers who were sent a 2010/11 Tax Return.
28 February 2012	First automatic 5% surcharge imposed for failing to pay tax due for 2010/11.	Late payers of tax for 2010/11.

20 2010 AND 2011 BUDGET MEASURES

Since the 2010 Edition of this guide was published:

- there has been a General Election leading to the formation of a Conservative/Liberal Democrat Coalition Government; and

- there have been two Budgets, in June 2010 and March 2011.

All the major tax changes set out in these two Budgets, as well as others previously announced but taking effect from 6 April 2011, are set out in this chapter.

2011/12 Personal allowances

	£
Personal	
aged under 65	*7,475
aged 65–74	**9,940
aged 75 and over	**10,090
Married Couples	
aged 75 and over	***7,295
minimum amount	***2,800
Income limit for under 65	
personal allowance	100,000
Income limit for age-related allowances	24,000
Relief for blind person (each)	1,980

* The personal allowance reduces at the rate of £1 for every £2 of income in excess of £100,000.

** The personal and married couple's allowances come down by £1 for every £2 of income above the income limit of £24,000.

*** Indicates allowances where tax relief is restricted to 10%.

Tax rates and bands for 2011/12

Band of taxable income	Rate of tax	Tax on band	Cumulative Tax
£	%	£	£
0-35,000	20	7,000.00	7,000.00
35,001-150,000	40	46,000.00	53,000.00
Over 150,000	50		

A lower tax rate of 10% is charged on your savings income:

- of up to £2,560; but

- after taking off your personal allowance.

The rate of tax on dividend income within the higher rate band is 32.5%, increasing to 42.5% on dividend income taxable at the additional rate.

Rates of National Insurance contributions for 2011/12

Class 1 Contributions for Employees

Contributions levied on weekly earnings above £139 but which do not exceed £817	12%	10.4%
If weekly earnings exceed £817	2%	2%

Reduced rate for married women
and widows with a valid
Election Certificate: 5.85%

Men and women over State Pension Age:
Nil

Earnings Threshold	Weekly	£139
	Monthly	£602
	Annually	£7,225
Upper earnings limit	Weekly	£817
	Monthly	£3,540
	Annually	£42,475

Class 2 contributions for the self-employed

Weekly flat rate	£2.50
Small Earnings Exception	£5,315

Class 3 Voluntary Contributions

Weekly rate	£12.60

Class 4 Contributions for the self-employed

on profits between £7,225 and £42,475: 9%

on profits in excess of £42,475: 2%

Child and Working Tax Credits

The rates for 2011/12 of both the Child and Working Tax Credits are as follows:

Child Tax Credit

	£
Family element	545
Child element (each child)	2,555
Disabled child element	2,800
Severe disability element	1,130

Working Tax Credit

Basic entitlement	1,920
Additional couples and lone parent element	1,950
30 hour element	790
Disability element	2,650
Severe disability element	1,130
50 plus return to work payment, for 16-29 hours	1,365
50 plus return to work payment, for 30-plus hours	2,030

Child care element

Maximum eligible cost for two or more children	£300 per week
Maximum eligible cost for one child	£175 per week
Percentage of eligible cost covered	70%

For 2011/12:

- Tax credits will taper away at a rate of 41% for each £1 of family income over the first income threshold of £6,420 (£15,860 when no Working Tax Credit is claimed).

- The second withdrawal percentage, which determines the rate at which the family element of Child Tax Credit is tapered, is also 41% based on on income threshold of £40,000.

Company Car Tax

Where a car is made available for an employee's private use there is a tax charge based on the percentage of the list price of the car, but graduated according to the level of the car's carbon dioxide (CO_2) emissions. From 6 April 2011:

- The £80,000 price cap for calculating the car benefit is abolished;

- The lower threshold CO_2 emissions figure is reduced to 125g/km;

- The "appropriate percentage" applicable to electric cars registered from 1998 comes down from 15% to 9%; and

- The reductions for electric/petrol hybrid cars and those fuelled by bio-fuel/road fuel gas and bioethanol are abolished.

Company Car Fuel Benefit

From 6 April 2011 the multiplier to be applied in working out the taxable benefit on fuel used for private motoring increases from £18,000 to £18,800.

Mileage Allowances

When employees use their own car on business they are not taxed on mileage allowances paid by their employers within approved rates. From 6 April 2011 the rate for the first 10,000 miles of business use goes up from 40p to 45p.

Child Care

From 6 April 2011 the £55 per week relief for child care will be capped so as to restrict the Income Tax relief for higher and additional rate taxpayers to that available to basic rate taxpayers.

Pensions

From 6 April 2011:

- The Annual Allowance on pension contributions qualifying for tax relief is reduced from £255,000 to £50,000.

- Higher and additional rate tax relief will be available in full on pension contributions within the qualifying limit.

- Any unused part of the £50,000 Annual Allowance can be carried forward for up to three tax years.

The Lifetime Allowance remains at £1.8m until 6 April 2012 when it is expected to fall.

Furnished Holiday Accommodation

The main changes from 6 April 2011 to the tax regime relating to the letting of furnished holiday accommodation are:

- Losses arising from the letting can only be carried forward against future profits of the same furnished holiday letting business.

- They can no longer be offset against other income.

Individual Savings Accounts

For 2011/12 the maximum annual amount that can be invested by all qualifying individuals is £10,680 of which no more than £5,340 can go into cash.

With the launch of Junior ISAs parents will be able to save for their children's futures. The accounts, designed as a replacement for Child Trust Funds:

- will be available from the autumn in 2011;
- to children under 18 who do not have an existing Child Trust Fund account.

Enterprise Investment Scheme

From 6 April 2011 the rate of Income Tax relief on qualifying investments under the Enterprise Investment Scheme goes up from 20% to 30%.

Value Added Tax

The Value Added Tax registration threshold is increased with effect from 1 April 2011 from taxable turnover of £70,000 to £73,000. The cancellation of registration limit goes up from £68,000 to £71,000.

New fuel scale charges for businesses with prescribed accounting periods starting on or after 1 May 2011 have been issued.

Capital Gains Tax

For 2011/12:

- The Capital Gains Tax exemption limit is increased to £10,600; and
- The lifetime allowance on gains qualifying for Entrepreneurs' Relief goes up from £5m to £10m

Inheritance Tax

The Nil rate band remains at £325,000.

Looking to the future

Some of the measures announced will not take effect immediately.

Measure	Date of introduction
The Personal Allowance is increased to £8,105, accompanied by a reduction in the limit of income taxable at the basic rate to £34,370.	6 April 2012
Late-night taxi rides provided by employers to their employees when they work late will become a taxable benefit-in-kind.	6 April 2012
The limit on expenditure qualifying for the Annual Investment Limit for capital allowances comes down from £100,000 to £25,000. Also the general and special rates of writing down allowances reduce from 20% and 10% to 18% and 8% respectively.	6 April 2012
Under the rules dealing with the taxation of furnished holiday accommodation the period that a property is actually let will be increased from 70 to 105 days per annum. Furthermore the amount of time that the property is actually available for letting will go up from 140 to 210 days per annum.	6 April 2012
The maximum annual sum an individual can invest under the Enterprise Investment Scheme and qualify for the various tax reliefs goes up from £500,000 to £1m.	6 April 2012
Non-domiciliaries who have been resident in the UK for 12 or more years will become liable to an annual charge of £50,000, up from £30,000, in order to claim the remittance basis.	6 April 2012
A reduced (36%) rate of Inheritance Tax will apply where 10% or more of a deceased's net Estate (after deducting exemptions, reliefs and the Nil rate band) is left to charity.	6 April 2012
The current rules for determining whether an individual is UK resident for tax purposes are unclear and largely based on a century's worth of case law. The Government has announced a period of consultation with the intention of introducing a simpler statutory test.	6 April 2012

Measure	Date of introduction
At present the various tax allowances, the annual Individual Savings Account subscription limit, the annual exemption limit for Capital Gains Tax and the various limits and thresholds for the payment of National Insurance contributions increase each year by reference to the movement in the Retail Price Index. It is intended that future changes will be measured by the movement in the Consumer Price Index.	6 April 2012
The relevant percentages for taxing company cars will be reduced by 1% for cars with carbon emissions between 95g/km to 220g/km.	6 April 2013
The 50% top rate of tax to be axed.	By 2015
Income Tax and National Insurance to be merged.	By 2015

Lightning Source UK Ltd.
Milton Keynes UK
UKOW051507260412

191519UK00001B/303/P